AGAINST THE TIDE

Against the Tide

HOW A COMPLIANT CONGRESS EMPOWERED A RECKLESS PRESIDENT

■

Lincoln Chafee

THOMAS DUNNE BOOKS

ST. MARTIN'S PRESS

New York

THOMAS DUNNE BOOKS.
An imprint of St. Martin's Press.

AGAINST THE TIDE. Copyright © 2008 by Lincoln Chafee.
All rights reserved. Printed in the United States of America.
No part of this book may be used or reproduced in any manner whatsoever
without written permission except in the case of brief quotations
embodied in critical articles or reviews. For information, address
St. Martin's Press, 175 Fifth Avenue, New York, N.Y. 10010.

www.thomasdunnebooks.com
www.stmartins.com

Design by Victoria Hartman

"There Will Be Peace in the Valley for Me"
by Thomas A. Dorsey, © 1939 (renewed)
Warner-Tamerlane Publishing Corp.
All rights reserved. Used by permission of Alfred Publishing Co., Inc.

ISBN-13: 978-0-312-38304-6
ISBN-10: 0-312-38304-5

First Edition: April 2008

10 9 8 7 6 5 4 3 2 1

For John Chafee,
a brave Marine,
honest public servant,
and a superb father

■

Contents

Acknowledgments

Much of the material in this book is taken from my discussions with students in the classrooms and halls of Brown University, where I am a visiting fellow at the Watson Institute for International Studies. Many students have come up to me after these events, saying, "You should tell this story in a book." It seemed a daunting task then, but now many long days at the keyboard are forgotten in the pleasure of seeing the book in final form.

It was not have been possible without the love, understanding, and good humor of my wife, Stephanie, and our children, Louisa, Caleb, and Thea. They cheerfully lived many of the events recounted in these pages.

I would not have been able to devote the time necessary without the support of Ruth Simmons, president of Brown University; Barbara Stallings, director of the Watson Institute; Geoffrey Kirkman, associate director; and Miranda Fasulo, executive assistant. Geoffrey went the extra mile, adding to his own busy workload by reading and commenting insightfully on the text.

Tony DePaul, a veteran newspaper reporter who helped me write the manuscript, brought professionalism and an easygoing nature to the project and a maniacal insistence that we meet every deadline. Matt Endreny was reliable and enthusiastic in checking the facts of my account against the public record. My brother, John Chafee, a writer and teacher who has always enjoyed a phrase well turned, was a careful reader and provided much guidance. Debbie Rich, my press secretary as mayor and senator, was always ready to come to my aid on a moment's notice. Catherine Taylor assisted me in writing on the important Middle East issues I address in the book and my sister-in-law Lee Chafee helped with a final review of the manuscript.

A fellow Brown graduate, John Silbersack, executive vice president of Trident Media Group, and his assistant, Libby Kellogg, were of great help in representing my proposal to publishers.

I'll be ever grateful to my publisher, Thomas Dunne Books, for deciding that the project had merit. I liked Tom Dunne immediately when we met in May 2007 in New York, and I was delighted that he wanted to comment on the manuscript and work with me before sending it on to his team of editors. I enjoyed working with Senior Editor Rob Kirkpatrick, Rob's assistant, Lorrie McCann, and Associate Editor Kathleen Gilligan. They were always patient with the many questions that a first-time author tends to ask.

AGAINST THE TIDE

1

A STIFF DOSE OF TRUTH

In the decades before the seismic congressional elections of 1994, two dozen moderate Republican senators would meet for lunch in the U.S. Capitol every Wednesday to build camaraderie, enjoy one another's company, and talk about how they would work together in the week to come. They represented states in every corner of America and believed in conserving natural resources, protecting individual liberties, confronting foreign nations only when it served the national interest, using the tools of government to help our most vulnerable citizens, and raising enough revenue to cover spending.

By 1999, when I became the Republican senator from Rhode Island, the party had drifted so far right that only five Republicans were willing to be seen at the moderates' table on Wednesdays. We had no one there from, say, Wyoming or Kansas anymore. Our most senior member was Arlen Specter of Pennsylvania. Like me, the rest were New Englanders:

Olympia Snowe and Susan Collins of Maine, and James Jeffords of Vermont, who would later quit the party to become an Independent.

The real action was at the Conservative Steering Committee, which had probably started out at a table for five and then grew to include almost the entire Republican caucus. The Senate delegation from the South was inexorably turning from conservative Democrat to conservative Republican, and the hard-liners solidified their gains when they took over the House and the Senate in 1994, two years into President Bill Clinton's first term. The Republicans who came out of the House and were elected to the Senate that year had chafed under Democratic rule and were eager to flex their muscles as the new majority.

Early in December 2000, Senator Specter asked Richard Cheney, our Republican vice presidential candidate, to have lunch with us on Wednesday, December 13. The vote-counting fiasco in Florida was under way, and no one knew whether Texas governor George W. Bush or Vice President Al Gore had been elected the nation's forty-third president. Then, the night before we were to meet with Mr. Cheney, the news broke: The U.S. Supreme Court had declared the Florida recount unconstitutional. The Court authorized Katherine Harris, Florida's Republican secretary of state, to declare Bush and Cheney victorious.

We Republicans had won the presidency by a single vote in the Electoral College and a single vote in the Supreme Court. In the executive branch, winning by a whisker is as good as winning in a landslide, but not so in the Senate. For the first time in a century we had a Senate split down the middle, fifty-

fifty, with a Republican vice president available to break a tie in our favor. That whisker-thin margin of victory had real consequences, to my way of thinking.

It meant that our small club of five moderate Republican votes would be vital to President-elect Bush if he had any hope of getting his legislative initiatives through.

Despite that happy turn of events—happy for us moderates, I thought—I was sure Richard Cheney would have more important things to do that following noon than keep his appointment with our lonely band of five.

I was wrong about that, and more.

I made my way through a rabbit warren of corridors to Senator Specter's office, actually a satellite of his main office, and so well hidden in the Capitol we called it "the hideaway." Hidden or not, I found a crowd of reporters and photographers and, in the middle of that crush, our new vice president-elect. I was surprised and delighted to see him there and felt I was a witness to history in the making. George Bush had promised to bring America together again, and here was his running mate holding out his hand to the key moderate votes the president-elect would need to keep that promise. What a humbling experience it must be for Mr. Cheney, I thought, as I watched him navigate the press gauntlet: to lose the popular vote but come to power with a one-vote margin in the Electoral College after a historic Supreme Court ruling.

President-elect Bush had made a solemn promise to be "a uniter, not a divider." That resonated after six years of sniping and bickering between the White House and the Congress, led by Speaker of the House Newt Gingrich. In the Senate, Majority Leader Bob Dole had the unenviable task of trying to keep the new breed of fire-breathing Republicans in line. On June 12, 1996, after less than two years, the job went to Trent Lott of Mississippi, who relished partisan battle.

Soon the country would endure the seamy and embarrassing spectacle of the impeachment proceedings against President Clinton. It was a sickening discord that seemed to go on and on without end. The American people and many in Congress were thirsting for the different approach that George Bush had promised in 2000.

In my first year in the Senate, I dreaded going to the moderates' Wednesday lunches because we never seemed to get past complaining about the insignificant role the Republican caucus allowed us to play in shaping legislation. I have never been big on moaning and whining. *Oh, woe is us. We have no power. Our Republican leaders don't listen. They just do what they want . . .* If we had beer we would have cried in it, but this was lunch. I called it the weekly "crying in our soup." But there would be no more of that with the Senate divided right down the middle, I thought. We were the five moderate voices that could tip a partisan vote one way or the other, which meant they would have to become less partisan. We could get control of the agenda and change the tone in Washington. It was clearly what the country needed and wanted, a move to the center and some measurable progress on some vital issues, particularly: the environment, health care, tax fairness. Three of us around the table, Jeffords, Snowe, and I, had a fresh mandate from the voters. We had been elected to new terms just a few weeks earlier. The voters had endorsed our occasional splits with the Republican leadership, times when we voted with President Clinton on health and workplace issues that affected their daily lives for the better. All three of us had won by comfortable margins. It was no fluke, because the opposite was true for conservative Republican incumbents and conservative challengers alike. The voters had battered them in race after race. Five incumbent Republican senators had gone down in defeat, all loyal to the right-wing agenda of our leadership team.

I had seen this sort of political dynamic before, at home in Rhode Island. In the late 1980s, a small group of Republican senators controlled all legislation that passed through the heavily Democratic State Senate. At the time, Democrats held forty-one of fifty seats in the Rhode Island Senate. They promptly split into subparties, as can happen when you have an overwhelming majority. People who think politically start to break up into cliques as they feud over how to gain control of the megaparty. Democratic loyalties in Rhode Island were split between Senator John Bevilacqua and Senator David Carlin. The Bevilacqua faction ran the Senate by one vote, as long as it could win over every Republican. No piece of legislation was adopted unless it addressed the concerns of Minority Leader Bob Goldberg and his tiny band of swing votes.

In 2001, I told this bit of Rhode Island lore to my fellow Republican moderates in the U.S. Senate. I argued that we could do the same in a Senate where the right and the left were split fifty-fifty. Nothing could pass without the moderates' support *if* we stuck together.

The administration had a plan for making sure we did not stick together. That was why Richard Cheney came to our lunch that day: Not to say he needed us, but to tell us that he and George W. Bush were in charge and no one else.

The reporters were ushered out, the door was closed, and there sat the six of us, not a staff member in sight. We made a little small talk at first. The vice president recalled that he and my father, the late U.S. senator John H. Chafee, had gone on a pack trip in bear country in the 1980s when the federal government was hearing testimony on listing the grizzly bear as an endangered species. At the time, Mr. Cheney represented Wyoming in the House.

Soon we got down to business, and that was when Richard Cheney would shatter everything I had believed was true about our party, our campaign, our victory, and the four years ahead.

In steady, quiet tones, the vice president-elect laid out a shockingly divisive political agenda for the new Bush administration, glossing over nearly every pledge the Republican ticket had made to the American voter. We were going to get out of a host of international agreements, he said. We would disavow the United Nations' Kyoto Protocol on global climate change, even if it were to be ratified by a sufficient number of nations to give it the force of international law. We would end our support for the establishment of the International Criminal Court in The Hague. We would cancel the Anti-Ballistic Missile Treaty ratified in 1972. We would slash taxes by $1.6 trillion and wipe out the budget surpluses generated in the Clinton era. John Ashcroft of Missouri, defeated in his Senate reelection bid weeks earlier because voters rejected his far-right politics, was being seriously discussed as our next attorney general. I like John Ashcroft. We were always on friendly terms, but he would be a polarizing choice for attorney general at this critical time when we had an opportunity, at last, to heal a fractured Congress.

President-elect Bush had promised that healing, but now we moderate Republicans were hearing Richard Cheney articulate the real agenda: a clashist approach on every issue, big and small, and any attempt at consensus would be a sign of weakness. We would seek confrontation on every front. He said nothing about education or the environment or health care; it was all about these new issues that were rarely, if ever, touted in the campaign. The new administration would divide Americans into red and blue, and divide nations into those who stand with us or against us. I knew that what Mr. Cheney was saying would rip the closely divided Congress apart. We moderates had often voted with President Clinton on things that powerful Republican constituencies didn't like: an increase in the minimum wage, a patients' bill of rights, and campaign finance reform. Mr. Cheney knew this, but he ticked off the issues at the top of his agenda and did it fearlessly. It made no difference to him that we were potential adversaries; he was going down his to-do list and checking off Confrontation Number 1.

Senator Arlen Specter spoke first. As the most junior member, I would have my say last, if at all. I could hardly sit still as I waited to hear my respected friend wade into this outrageous manifesto.

And then, in a moment I can only describe as infuriating, Senator Specter took no leadership role in representing the moderate point of view. He acquiesced, and others followed his example.

As each of my colleagues spoke in turn, I waited for one of them to push back. Surely one of them would have the presence of mind to say, *Whoa! Time-out! What are you talking about, Mister Vice President? You weren't elected to scrap international agreements. You never said to the voters: Elect us and we promise to bring back deficit spending and drive the next generation into debt.*

But no one resisted. We sat there and listened as Mr. Cheney made divisive pronouncements of policy that would come as a complete surprise to many of the Americans who had voted to elect the Bush-Cheney ticket. I stopped waiting for someone to challenge Mr. Cheney when I saw my Republican friends around the table nodding in agreement as he held forth.

I was at a loss to explain my colleagues' compliant behavior then. I remain so now. It may have been an all-too-human response to the circumstances of the time. Anxious weeks of uncertainty were finally over. Now we knew the outcome of the election. The bitterness of the Florida recount was behind us. My colleagues seemed happy and relieved just to know who was in charge. And they seemed a little awestruck. *This is the vice president of the United States.*

The contentious and destructive agenda that Mr. Cheney dropped on us was troubling enough, but what really unnerved me was his attitude. He welcomed conflict. We Republicans had promised America exactly the opposite. In the presidential debates, moderator Jim Lehrer asked Governor Bush to describe the foreign policy he would adopt, if elected. Candidate Bush said he would be humble in foreign affairs; that if we were arrogant, other countries would resent us. Now his running mate was telling us the new administration would make a *point* of being arrogant and divisive. Mr. Cheney was brazen in his pronouncements. *A humble foreign policy?* His attitude was anything but humble. He said that the campaign was over and that our actions in office would not be dictated by what had to be said in the campaign. And he pronounced this deception with no emotion or window dressing of any kind. He was fearless, matter of fact, and smug.

I wondered, where does Cheney get the nerve to say these things a few hours after the Court established him as our vice president-elect? Where did he get the authority to make this radical departure from the president-elect's own campaign rhetoric?

I had supported Governor George W. Bush over Senator John McCain in the 2000 Rhode Island presidential primary. I met the Texas governor for the first time in 1999, when he came to Rhode Island to raise money. I contributed and sincerely applauded his remarks to supporters at the Providence Convention Center. He had good campaign patter, and I was impressed. He said all the right things. I thought he could win on his pledge to bring a new, unifying atmosphere to Washington, and that he might even be as good and decent a president as his father had been. He seemed moderate enough to win support from all sides, and he had the Bush name. After the bitter partisan atmosphere of the Clinton impeachment, voters looked back with affection at the governor's father.

I liked that the governor had worked cooperatively with Democrats in the Texas legislature. If leaders in both parties could rally around him, he was just what the country needed. America stood at the summit of power, emerging from the cold war as an economic, cultural, and military force without equal. We had wasted valuable years in partisan bickering, but our moment in history was still at hand.

What a tremendous opportunity and responsibility to do good things in the world.

Then came that devastating first day after George W. Bush and Richard Cheney prevailed in the Supreme Court. If we were to believe Mr. Cheney, the president-elect would not only reignite the partisanship of the Clinton-Gingrich era but would make it even more toxic. Mr. Cheney tore our best campaign promises to shreds and the moderates acquiesced instead of pelting him with outrage. It was clear to me then that there would be no key bloc of moderate votes helping to shape legislation and reunite America over the next four years. In any event, Cheney was not asking for support—he was ordering us to provide it. The president-elect had his agenda; we were just along for the ride.

My heart sank as my colleagues peeled away, one by one. It was the most demoralizing moment of my seven-year tenure in the Senate.

When it was my turn to speak, I made the case that our five votes would be crucially important in an evenly divided Senate. I chose my words carefully, and probably stammered with the effort to contain my fury. We were on the cusp of a new millennium that held enormous promise for American leadership in the world, and what I had just heard was petty, arrogant, and irresponsible. It threatened to lead in exactly the wrong direction.

I spoke in the perhaps too-optimistic hope that I might yet rally the moderates to seriously apprehend the implications of the new agenda. When I told Mr. Cheney, "Our votes at this table are important," he could hardly be bothered. He gave me the back of his hand with a truism: "Every vote is important."

There was no support to be had, and lunch was over.

I was more than unhappy as I walked back to my office in the Russell Senate Office Building, disgusted with the vice president for his audacity and with my fellow moderates for the weakness they had shown. I thought back to the Republican convention in Philadelphia just six months earlier, in August, when I applauded Mr. Cheney's speech. It was uplifting and emotionally charged, but that was before I knew the Bush administration would be so willing to use words dishonestly.

Mr. Cheney recalled for the convention his days as secretary of defense, describing his frequent helicopter flights over Washington and how he looked down on the city with thoughts that were solemn, patriotic, and reverent.

"When you make that trip from Andrews to the Pentagon, and you look down on the city of Washington, one of the first things you see is the Capitol, where all the great debates that have shaped two hundred years of American history have taken place.

"You fly down along the Mall and see the monument to George Washington, a structure as grand as the man himself. To the north is the White House, where John Adams once prayed 'that none but honest and wise men [may] ever rule under this roof.'

"Next you see the memorial to Thomas Jefferson, the third president and the author of our Declaration of Independence. And then you fly over the memorial to Abraham Lincoln, this greatest of presidents, the man who saved the Union.

"Then you cross the Potomac, on approach to the Pentagon. But just before you settle down on the landing pad, you look upon Arlington National Cemetery, its gentle slopes and crosses row on row.

"I never once made that trip without being reminded how enormously fortunate we all are to be Americans, and what a terrible price thousands have paid so that all of us, and millions more around the world might live in freedom."

A day later, I was jolted to read that the staff at Arlington National Cemetery had put out a statement correcting something our candidate for vice president had said in the most inspiring part of his address.

The cemetery staff took note of the reference to "gentle slopes and crosses, row on row," and noted: "There are no crosses in Arlington National Cemetery."

They suggested that Mr. Cheney had lifted the image from "In Flanders Field," a moving poem by Canadian John McCrae, in 1915.

In Arlington National Cemetery the American war dead of all faiths lie under tombstones with rounded tops.

Richard Cheney, who avoided military service as a young man, may never have looked out the helicopter window as secretary of defense to reflect solemnly on the sacrifice of the fallen.

Did he think it was all right to push that emotional button for political gain? To use America's war dead as a campaign prop?

The cemetery staff stood up for the truth and held Mr. Cheney to account. This was no partisan press release; it came from the professionals who see our war dead to their final resting places, and who work under the motto "Where Valor Proudly Sleeps." They resented that Richard Cheney had made up a tender story about the hallowed grounds they tend, or had allowed a Republican National Committee speech-writer to make one up for him.

If he was willing to speak falsely about Arlington National Cemetery, what else in his speech would prove inaccurate?

Given that this was a campaign event, Mr. Cheney sang hosannas not just to America, but to the integrity and wisdom of our nominee, the Texas governor, saying he had "the courage, and the vision, and the goodness, to be a great president."

"I see in our nominee the qualities of mind and spirit our nation needs, and our history demands," he said. "Big changes are coming to Washington. To serve with this man, in this cause, is a chance I would not miss.

"George W. Bush will repair what has been damaged. He is a man without pretense and without cynicism. A man of principle, a man of honor. On the first hour of the first day he will restore decency and integrity to the Oval Office. He will show us that national leaders can be true to their word and that they can get things done by reaching across the partisan aisle, and working with political opponents in good faith and common purpose.

"In this election, they will speak endlessly of risk; we will speak of progress. They will make accusations; we will make proposals. They will feed fear; we will appeal to hope. They will offer more lectures and legalisms and carefully worded denials; we offer another way, a better way, and a stiff dose of truth."

At the time I had been in the Senate for a year and had witnessed the hard-right agenda at work, but I must admit I was caught up in the spirit of the convention and honestly thought this was one of the most rousing political speeches I had heard in years.

After the revelations of the Wednesday lunch four months later, my head was swimming with the vice president-elect's pronouncements on Republican policy, his assertion that everything we had said in the campaign was about campaigning and winning and getting power. They had a whole different plan for governing.

I take people at their word. When someone abuses my trust and proves his word false, I am forever on my guard. I made a commitment then and there to be on guard with this new administration. That determination would serve me well over the next six years when voting on the Bush-Cheney agenda.

When I got back to my office that day, I told my chief of staff, David Griswold, that I had been briefed on the Republican postelection platform and was deeply alarmed. I had worked to elect the Bush-Cheney ticket thinking we would do great things together if Republicans should win the White House. Now I was so rattled by what Mr. Cheney had said—and how he had said it—I was moved to sit down and address a letter to him right away. I wanted to get it on paper that we had made a commitment, as candidates, to unite the nation and not divide it.

In that letter, I wrote:

> The following are some issues I believe bode well for success:
>
> *Debt Reduction*—We are on an encouraging course toward reducing the national debt, and I believe we must maintain discipline both in discretionary spending and in proposals for significant tax cuts. This time of relative

prosperity and peace is an opportune time to eliminate the debt. As you know, *interest payments* on the debt still consume a staggering proportion of the federal budget—amounting to $222 billion in Fiscal Year 2000.

Tax Fairness—Majorities from both parties in Congress expressed support in the past year for reform of the estate tax and repeal of the so-called marriage tax penalty. This appears to be an area of great promise for early bipartisan cooperation. Democrats can be expected to support reform in both these areas at least to the extent contained in the substitute amendments proposed this past summer by the fiscally responsible Senator Moynihan.

Education—I hope that common ground can be identified on a package to reauthorize the Elementary and Secondary Education Act. I believe our chief emphasis in federal education policy should be funding for the Individuals with Disabilities Education Act. As you know, IDEA was enacted with the goal that the federal government would compensate local school districts for 40 percent of the cost of compliance. Instead, federal support languishes at about 15 percent, while local districts struggle to comply with this worthwhile but costly law. I hope we can make significant progress in making good on the federal commitment.

Health Care—The debate over prescription drug coverage in Medicare and reform of managed care through a Patients' Bill of Rights collapsed amid partisan wrangling this year. But these issues will continue to stir public interest, and proposals do exist that provide measured steps with bipartisan support. I look forward to working with you to help shape an approach that the new administration might support.

Environment—Progress on environmental issues could do much to enhance the new administration's program, and a first step could be enactment of legislation I have sponsored to advance the cleanup of abandoned urban "brownfields," both to speed the redevelopment of these properties and to preserve the environment. There is wide bipartisan support for this legislation and I hope it can be made part of your agenda. In addition, I hope the new administration will be open to proposals to reduce the country's reliance on foreign oil, through energy conservation and greater investments in mass transit.

The agenda Mr. Cheney had outlined at lunch was certain to tear the country apart. My letter to him was fair warning; I would not be a soldier in his cause.

2

WARWICK POLITICS 101

The Republican Party of George W. Bush did not suddenly spring into being in November 2000. Its roots go back to 1964, the year the Democratic South cast its electoral votes for Senator Barry Goldwater, a determined opponent of the Civil Rights Act. I was eleven when Republicans nominated the Arizona senator for president, but old enough to know he was on the wrong side of history. My father, Rhode Island governor John H. Chafee, had been asked to speak at the convention that year, in San Francisco. On the train ride west, he worked on his speech while my older brother, Zech, and I had the run of the California Zephyr. Like the late president John F. Kennedy, my father, a marine who fought on Guadalcanal and Okinawa, was one of a new generation of political leaders to come out of World War II. He was hoping to see his Republican Party nominate one of our moderate eastern governors, William Scranton of Pennsylvania or Nelson Rockefeller of New York. Rockefeller was controversial.

He was the leader of a new wave of Republican governors who embraced social programs as a way to build the middle class. Mark Hatfield in Oregon, Charles Percy in Illinois, John Volpe in Massachusetts, and my father in Rhode Island were among this new generation of forward-looking Republican governors, the "Rockefeller Republicans." At the convention in the Cow Palace, I watched in fascination as the delegates booed Rockefeller long and loud. They were fervently against where he wanted to take the Grand Old Party. Finally, Rockefeller turned in exasperation to the chairman, Senator Thruston Morton of Kentucky, and said, "You quiet them down." The Republicans on the floor were having fun booing Rockefeller, and I was riveted in the witnessing of it. When I got a little older, I realized what that was all about: Rockefeller was trying to take the party down the center, and the old-line Republican faithful were digging in to resist. Their man, Senator Barry Goldwater, stood for unchanging tradition, a view of government so limited that even the Civil Rights Act was meddlesome legislation. It made no difference that everyone at the convention knew he had little chance of winning the presidency. Being right was more important than winning. They loved Goldwater because he championed a brand of personal moral rectitude that had no patience with the failings of others. He stood for no compromise, ever, with anyone. Declaring that "Extremism in the defense of liberty is no vice," he was for an aggressive, interventionist foreign policy. President Lyndon Johnson beat the Arizona senator in a landslide, but the seeds of the new Republican Party had been planted in the South, and the region started voting Republican in congressional races. Senators Strom Thurmond and Jesse Helms, both former Democrats, were the first far-right Republicans the South elected. Two generations later, during my Senate tenure, Senator Zell Miller of Georgia would be the region's last far-right Democrat, so far right he shunned his own candidate and gave a fiery speech at the 2004 *Republican* convention. The change was complete. By the 1990s, southern Republicans had a lock on congressional leadership, and the moderating influence of the Alan Simpsons, Howard Bakers, and Nancy Kassebaums had faded into memory.

In March 1999, my father announced that he would not seek a fifth term as the U.S. senator from Rhode Island. I decided to run for the open seat and started the arduous task of raising the millions it would take to succeed. Then, that fall, everything changed overnight. My father died unexpectedly, and Governor Lincoln Almond asked me to go to Washington to serve the year remaining in his term. At the time, I was mayor of Warwick, Rhode Island, a city of ninety thousand on scenic Greenwich Bay. I had governed successfully for seven years as the All-But-Lone Republican. My party never held more than two of the nine seats on the city council. We had our battles, but Democrats knew I was fair and kept my word and that I respected them. Carlo Pisaturo, my Democratic council president and a rival for my job, once honored me by telling a reporter, on the record, "His word is gold." On the whole, our two branches of government made Warwick a better city by negotiating differences and, in most cases, cooperating once we had ironed them out as best we could. I was eager to work that way in Washington, one of only five former mayors in the U.S. Senate, and, I was sure, the only senator who had spent his twenties shoeing horses in Kentucky and

Montana and on the Canadian prairie. I had grown up at a dinner table where we talked politics and was not naive about how things worked in Washington. I knew what pitched partisan battles were all about, from my own experience and that of my father when, as a Republican governor, he had to deal with the Democratic Rhode Island General Assembly. Bound for Washington, I was determined to apply my work ethic and political skills and, if I could, make things better. I never had any use for partisan bickering for its own sake and did not plan to fit in, if that was the way to fit in. I would never apologize to a fellow Republican for voting moderate to liberal on social issues, and would not associate only with Democrats, even if conservative Republicans and right-wing pundits thought I should. The great history of my party belongs to me, not just to the newcomers who changed it into the Old Dixie club. I went to Washington as a proud Republican, even if I did not think we should hang our hats on denying climate change, overturning *Roe v. Wade,* and wearing our righteousness on our sleeves and our patriotism on our lapels.

For anyone interested in serving their country in elective office, I highly recommend local politics as the best training ground. I may not have realized it in my early years as a city councilman, then mayor, but the lessons I learned in Warwick proved invaluable in Washington.

In 1985, I was settling into Rhode Island again after being away for seven years, practicing my blacksmithing trade. I was interested in politics and decided that, as a first-time candidate, an obscure first contest was in order: I would try to win a seat at the Rhode Island Constitutional Convention. I went to a printer and ordered eight thousand palm cards with my picture on the front, a slogan, and on the back a few words about where I went to school and the kind of work I had done, and then I went into the neighborhoods to campaign. Suddenly, I felt a wave of panic. I had had more equine than human company for seven cold and dark Alberta winters, paying my way by welding borium cleats on the shoes of horses that would race over frozen tracks until spring. I parked my car and sat there for twenty minutes. Finally, I screwed up my courage. It would have been humiliating to go home with a stack of palm cards in my hand.

I picked a house, rang the bell, and a moment later a woman looked out at me with apprehension. *Oh, no, is he trying to sell me a vacuum cleaner? Does he want to change my religion?* I smiled, held up a card, told her my name and asked her to support me as a delegate to the convention. Her face brightened into a wide smile of relief. There was nothing to buy, no religious conversion needed. I thought, *I can do this eight thousand times!* I had a new enthusiasm as I walked every street in the district and went on to win election as a delegate to the Constitutional Convention.

That gave me the confidence to run for city council in 1986, a much more demanding kind of race. My opponent, an incumbent Democrat, knew how to campaign. He had signs everywhere. Despite having grown up in a political family, I had no idea how important signs were, how to get them, or that there are ordinances governing where and when you can put them up. I was, in short, unprepared. I ran out to order signs and lost a few anxious weeks waiting for the printer to deliver them. When, at last, I tore into the packages of signs hot off the press I found my name misspelled: "Chaffee." That meant more days of waiting. In the meantime, my opponent's name was everywhere I looked, and my Chaffee signs were in the landfill. I thought, *Don't worry about signs. Just knock on more doors than he does.* It was more work than you might imagine, but I had always been curious about what was around the next turn in the road. I enjoyed wondering what kind of house I might find at the end of a long driveway. I was out meeting people as life at that moment found them. When there was a big football game on TV, I would follow the game from house to house.

I defeated the incumbent councilman, took the oath of office, and made a little notoriety for myself at my very first public hearing. The Warwick City Council was hearing evidence on a zone change proposed in historic Pawtuxet Village, where, on June 9, 1772, American colonists seized and burned the British packet ship HMS *Gaspee* after it ran aground while chasing *Hannah,* which had evaded British taxes on Narragansett Bay. In the spirit of those rebellious colonists, I led the charge for the neighborhood while most other city council members openly sided with the developer. One councilman actually referred to the developer's expert witness on traffic patterns as "our traffic man." The neighbors were furious.

When that raucous meeting ended after 1:00 A.M., I sat at my kitchen table and wrote a scathing indictment of the Democrats, accusing them of showing contempt for ordinary citizens and cozying up to rich developers who had campaign money to spread around. The article was printed the next day in the *Warwick Beacon.*

When we met again a week later, the Democrats let me have it with both barrels. Council president George Carberry allowed each council member all the time he wanted to come down on me with the harshest language this side of the backstretch. At the time, Warwick Democrats *were* the government. You had to pay your dues and be a good soldier before you got the Democratic endorsement for city council. Having come up in that system, my Democratic colleagues all had sharp elbows and knew how to throw them. Bob McKay, a Teamster truck driver and probably the toughest Democrat on the council, shouted at me that night, "I am not a crook!"

Ken Wild branded me "immature." John DelGiudice accused me of imagining that I rode a white horse to council meetings.

Reporters, who love a good pile-on, scribbled furiously, grabbing every sensational quote the Democrats used on me. This went on for an hour.

When the meeting adjourned, reporters cornered me for a response while the Democrats, in a group, walked across the City Hall parking lot to Saccoccio's, a local watering hole. They liked to have a few beers and unwind after meetings. I took my time answering questions, then headed over to Saccoccio's myself. I was not about to be left out. When I walked up to the Democrats' table and looked around for an empty chair, there was a disbelieving and uncomfortable silence. John DelGiudice, who had really beaten me to a pulp at the meeting, suddenly bellowed, "Sit down!" The Democrats laughed, shoved a glass of beer at me, and started talking about all the "amateur mistakes" I had made that evening. I smiled and thought, *People will be on my side when they read the paper tomorrow.* We made our predictions on which quotes the newspapers would trumpet in the morning. Everyone thought that John's "white horse" line was a sure bet. We were all right; that quote and many others were in the next day's news coverage. A few weeks later the newspaper introduced me to a statewide audience in a Sunday feature that said, "He doesn't look tough. Or particularly serious. He just doesn't fit the image of a maverick, a Republican challenging a comfortable Democratic establishment, an environmentalist crusading to save parts of one of the state's most heavily developed cities. . . . At 33 he looks like a shy, well-mannered college student. After one month in office, Chafee has emerged as a hard-hitter at the forefront of a burgeoning resident revolt against development."

MY DEMOCRATIC ADVERSARIES and I remained good friends for years afterward. The events of that evening taught me to fight hard, never let it fester, and never get frozen out. Years later, in the Senate, I found myself voting not against Democrats but my fellow Republicans. I always made a point of going to the next Republican event and sitting with the people who were stewing over something I had done or said.

Tension is natural in politics, but relationships can be repaired, and differences need not become personal.

I will say, though, that it is harder to use strong rhetoric against your own party. It was more fun at Warwick City Hall, where I was a member of the opposition. I was expected to be full-throated as I waded into the Democrats. In the U.S. Senate, you are expected to tone it down when you have strong disagreements with your own party. You show how you really feel behind closed doors, in caucus meetings. I always did, having learned how to stand up and be counted at the Warwick City Council. There I had taken all the abuse they could throw at me, and made my name as the only councilman who would go with the program when I thought the program was right and go my own way when I did not.

When my first term drew to a close in 1988, Democrats painted a bull's-eye on my back. Democratic mayor Frank Flaherty wanted me out and started funneling money and in-kind help into my challenger's campaign. I won only because the neighbors had seen me standing up for them while Democrats were slow to sense the growing public anger with overdevelopment.

Two years later, Mayor Flaherty ran for governor and I jumped at the chance to run for mayor. It was an open seat, my best opportunity to become the first Republican mayor in Warwick in thirty years.

It would not be possible to knock on every door in the city, so now I had to learn how to campaign through the mail and newspaper and radio ads. I needed every reform-minded voter on my side that year but would not get them. An independent candidate split the time-for-a-change vote, enabling Charles Donovan, the endorsed Democrat, to win with 46 percent to my 41 percent. Mayor Donovan lurched from one crisis to another over the next two years while I prepared for another run against him. He had made his name in the General Assembly as a staunch pro-labor Democrat, but once seated as mayor, an executive job, he always seemed to be waging some pitched battle with union firefighters, teachers, and sanitation workers.

On his watch, the schools were shut down in a series of teacher strikes, and by 1992 there was so much unrest in the city that Mayor Donovan knew his own party would oust him in a primary. He ran for a second term as an independent but would finish a distant third. The real fight that year was between me and the endorsed Democrat, Michael Brophy, my former colleague on the city council.

For many years, Mr. Brophy had been a good soldier, quietly awaiting his turn to run for mayor with the nod from the Democratic City Committee. But the old days were coming to a close. The winner of the Democratic primary was no longer guaranteed to prevail in the general election.

Rhode Island is arguably the most Democratic state in the country, but Republicans can get elected if they work hard enough. We were always taking on the entrenched Democratic Goliath that is the General Assembly. When I won by 335 votes out of 45,000 cast, former councilman Ken Wild, now chairman of the Democratic City Committee, smugly dismissed me as a fluke, a footnote, a pesky fly. He bragged that I would serve one term before the Democrats reunited behind a single candidate and swatted me with a rolled-up newspaper.

I will always believe that the very first executive decision I made as mayor was the thing that proved Ken Wild wrong two years later.

Everyone hired on the city payroll in the previous thirty-two years had come up through the Democratic patronage machine. There were *no* Republicans working in the Public Works Department, and I knew I would rise or fall on the success of that department because it touches the voters every day, filling potholes, picking up the garbage, and plowing the streets. With a two-year term I could not afford a single sloppy performance in a snowstorm.

Hiring a Public Works director was the most important decision I had to make. I wanted every employee there to be invested in making their boss look good, and that meant I had to hire a capable, well-liked Democrat.

His name was Ted Sheahan and I found him working right across the hall from my new office. He was Mayor Donovan's city clerk. Ted was jolly, larger than life, a big bald-headed man with a genius for making things happen, a positive thinker, and the people loved him. He relieved me of many day-to-day worries about the quality of services, and that freed me to work on solving Mayor Donovan's bitter labor dispute that was tearing apart our schools. I had only two Republican votes on the city council but the deal I brokered with the teachers' union was attractive enough to coax two Democrats and an independent to cross the partisan divide.

That first term had other challenges, too. In my first few weeks in office, a crew excavating for a new sewer line dislodged a natural gas pipe. Gas seeped through the ground into a family's home, fortunately unoccupied at the time. When the thermostat kicked on and made a spark, the house exploded into tons of kindling. A block away from the blast site boards were stuck like harpoons into houses and trees. It was a miracle that no one was killed.

With sewer construction crisscrossing the neighborhood, people were worried that their own houses might be next. How could they go to sleep at night knowing that if the improbable happened once it could happen again?

We had a meeting about it at the Pilgrim Senior Center, and the room was packed. We had the gas company and other experts at the head table, and I asked them to let the people vent. Residents were understandably frightened and angry, and I wanted us to listen and not say anything that would raise the pitch. The tone of the language *we* used had to be reassuring.

We would have other encounters like that in my tenure, over sewer assessments and airport noise, and I always made sure I stood up in front of the people and took the heat. I would explain my points as clearly as I could, and without confrontation. My supporters said, *Don't go to these things. Send low-level bureaucrats who don't have to stand for reelection.*

That struck me as not only poor leadership but poor politics. I would rather take a beating than be labeled a no-show. I wanted to explain my point of view and take my chances on winning people over as best I could. That is a huge part of the art of politics, and, more important, governing. I think Warwick people liked that I did business that way.

By 1994, I was tested, scarred, and comfortable as mayor, and that made me a tougher campaigner. Michael Brophy wanted a rematch of our close contest of two years earlier. This time I was the sitting mayor; I got out the brass knuckles and bloodied him. I like Mike Brophy and always will, but he was trying to bring back the Democratic machine and prove Ken Wild right about the "fluke" of my election in 1992. In our debates I demanded that he name just one accomplishment he had to his credit after many years on the school committee and city council. He never gave the voters an answer, let alone a good answer. That single question defined our race, in much the way that Ronald Reagan had defined his race against President Jimmy Carter by asking voters whether they were better off than four years earlier.

Hammering an opponent is a part of politics. I would never try to pretend that I was above it all. Voters want to know whether their candidates have a competitive heart and are willing to grapple. As the captain of my college wrestling team, I always was. You cannot hope to succeed in politics unless you are willing to be a scrapper when it counts. It helps to know when the time is right to land a blow, and at the same time how to stick to the issues and not make it personal. You have to score your points because no one else is going to score them for you.

In 1996, supporters urged me to run for Congress, for the open seat created when Representative Jack Reed declared for the Senate seat vacated by the retiring Claiborne Pell. But I was having too much fun being mayor. I made a positive difference for my city every day. Would I be able to say that as one of 435 members of the House of Representatives, a junior member at that?

I wanted a third term as my city's chief executive, and was sure I would win it in a walk—so sure that Democratic challenger George Zainyeh almost succeeded in handing me my unemployment papers.

I had forgotten a lesson I had learned in 1964, watching my father run for governor of Rhode Island: He paid attention to where his name appeared on the ballot that voters would face in the booth on election day. He was thinking strategically. He knew that few Rhode Islanders would ever vote for Republican Barry Goldwater as president. After they pulled the lever for President Johnson, my father needed them to get out of that Democratic column and look for him. His campaign ads drove home the message: *third column, fourth lever.* It worked. He got the overwhelmingly Democratic voters of Rhode Island to split their tickets and find the *third column, fourth lever.*

I faced the same problem thirty-two years later, in 1996, and it almost sidetracked my political aspirations.

On election night I had to sweat out the results at headquarters. I was losing districts that I should have been winning, losing entire wards that I should have been winning. I had polled extraordinarily well in the weeks leading up to the election, but those same people were voting for Democrat Bill Clinton over Republican Bob Dole, and then they were not hunting around in the Dole column for their incumbent Republican mayor, no matter how well Ted Sheahan had their street plowed.

I scraped by. Elected to a third term with a plurality in just three out of nine wards, I acquired an even greater respect that night for my father's wisdom and political savvy. I had gotten a little too comfortable in the big leather chair in the corner office; I needed a close call to teach me that elections can turn on the most mundane of mundane details: ballot placement. When my home ward, Ward 9, came through for me overwhelmingly and provided a narrow margin of victory citywide, my father said, "Isn't it gratifying that the people who know you best took the time to find you on the ballot and give you their support?"

It was indeed. But duly scared by the narrow win, I worked even harder for the next two years to accomplish things that would make this race my first landslide. I won with all nine wards in my column. But it was a term I would never complete.

When my father announced in 1999 that he would leave the Senate, he urged me to think carefully before running to succeed him. We talked about it one evening at the dining room table at my home on Warwick's Potowomut peninsula, bounded by the Greene River and Greenwich Bay.

Dad never urged me not to run, only to think twice. He recognized that, politically, the timing was good for me. "This is the window if you really want to do it," he said. "And if you're successful, be aware that the Senate life is hard on a young family." He was concerned about his grandchildren.

When Dad went to the Senate in 1976, his children were grown. In Washington, he met too many Senators who had hurt their families and missed out on so much by splitting their time between the District and their home states. The media has called the capital Divorce City because of the toll it takes on families.

Moreover, the job in Washington had changed, and not for the better, my father said. Things had never been so polarized in the World's Greatest Deliberative Body.

Politically, I knew it was time for me to move up or out. In Rhode Island, no Republican moves up unless the seat is open or the Democratic incumbent has been an absolute disaster. My father's retirement would be a rare opportunity for me to advance politically.

His advice to me was serious, and heartfelt.

There were sacrifices ahead for all, no doubt, but my family would never rank second to my desire to serve in the Senate. There was no danger of me getting a swelled head over a new title should I win. I knew that "United States Senator" would not affect my marriage or my relationship with my children.

My father gave me his best advice on both the personal and political dimensions of life in Washington. He saw that a rare chance was opening in Rhode Island for another Republican to go to the Senate, and I decided to step through it.

I will always feel sadness that Dad died before I won the race to succeed him. He died in office before he got to enjoy even a single day of the retirement he had announced. He had undergone back surgery in the summer of 1999, and though he returned to work in Washington I could see that he had never fully recovered. He died suddenly that October.

Assuming his duties by appointment made for a jarring transition. One day I was raising money and building support for my Senate run, the next day I was the incumbent senator. I went from thinking about firefighter contracts and snowstorms to explaining how I would vote on a national patients' bill of rights, the minimum wage, and gun safety.

I thought back to the night nine years earlier when I bucked Warwick's Democratic party bosses. I had a sense that, in Washington, I would end up bucking the Republican bosses who had radicalized my party's agenda. My father had pulled it off with seniority and a strong national record. His history in war and politics commanded respect. I was going in as the most junior of America's one hundred senators, and would be expected to fall in line.

3

LOYAL BULLFROGS

My first year in the Senate coincided with President Bill Clinton's final one in the White House. I was excited to be in Washington, proud to represent the center, as my father had done for twenty-three years, but I was eager to make my own name in national affairs and keep my job on my own strengths the following November. At the same time, I was dismayed at the bitterness I found in the Senate. It was worse than I expected. The atmosphere was one of trench warfare, two sides dug in, intent on destroying an enemy, and neither gaining any ground. In 2000, my colleagues and I had a lot on our plate, including health care, the minimum wage, tax fairness for married couples and small business owners, issues that most Americans thought were more important than the torturous drive to impeach President Clinton. The atmosphere was noxious. Majority Leader Trent Lott, the senator from Mississippi, worked hard to keep his "bullfrogs in the wheelbarrow," as he liked to say. The Democrats under Minority

Leader Tom Daschle were just as disciplined. They railed as one against our "Republican meanness," and I knew the label would get political traction in November if we had nothing to show for our efforts but a bitter stalemate.

When I took the oath of office in the United States Senate in November 1999, it was only my second time under the Capitol dome. My father had been a senator for more than two decades, but I rarely visited Washington and was as lost there as any out-of-towner. I had been out West plying my blacksmithing trade, then working in North Carolina for a year. When I returned to Rhode Island in 1985, I went to work at a steel mill in East Providence, then Electric Boat, the submarine builder. Finally, I was absorbed in my local political career in Warwick. Washington was virtually a new experience. It would be different, certainly. As mayor of Warwick, everything I did, every day, did something to make government run a little more efficiently for ninety thousand Warwick residents I deeply cared about. Now I was one lawmaker among many.

I left Stephanie, Louisa, Caleb, and Thea at our home in Warwick and found temporary quarters in the basement of my late father's house, in McLean, Virginia. Every day I drove his Ford Escort ten miles to his office and smiled whenever the air conditioner switched on and the car slowed down. The Escort was that underpowered. Dad was frugal, an old-school Yankee and a true New Englander. Fuel conservation and energy independence were daily decisions for him, not just world geopolitical issues.

It felt strange, even a little uncomfortable at first, to drive his car, park in his space, open the door to his office, work at his desk, sit in his chair in the Senate chamber. That seat befitted his seniority, not mine. The leadership decided there was no rush to put me in my rightful place, the far back corner of the chamber. If I won election to the Senate the following November, *then* I would be assigned a proper seat in Senate Siberia.

Naturally, those first days were difficult, just on an emotional level. The people who had worked for my father adored him, and they acquired stature in the Capitol by working for a long-serving committee chairman who was an authority on federal issues. Now they were working for me. Adoration, if any, would have to come a lifetime later. I made a common-sense decision not to change anything in the office and just do the best I could as a rookie Senator. My full-time job was to study, deliberate, and vote on the issues as the leadership brought them to the floor. My other full-time job was to raise millions and hit the campaign trail hard and try to get back to Washington in a year.

It was a demanding routine, and it left me little time to reflect on my personal loss or the city I had left behind.

The leadership appointed me to the Senate Foreign Relations Committee and the Environment and Public Works Committee. As chairman of the Foreign Relations Subcommittee on the Western Hemisphere, I would have to educate myself quickly on every important issue facing our relations with Canada and the whole of Latin America—the Caribbean, Mexico, Central America, and South America. When I heard that President Clinton was flying to Colombia for a series of diplomatic meetings, I wrangled an invitation. The White House told me to be at Andrews Air Force Base early the next morning; there would be a seat for me aboard Air Force One.

I bunked in the officers' quarters at Andrews that night and was standing on the tarmac at the crack of dawn. The president, notorious for being late, was late. As we waited, I chatted with lawmakers, cabinet members, and bureaucrats who were along for the ride. Attorney General Janet Reno was with us to help coordinate our antidrug efforts with her counterpart in Colombia. We landed at the airport outside Cartagena, on the Caribbean coast, then boarded the presidential motorcade for the ten- or twelve-mile ride into the city.

Tens of thousands of Colombians had gathered along the route to cheer our arrival. Mile after mile they stood, shoulder to shoulder and at least five deep. Some waved American flags, some just waved their arms. It was an apparently spontaneous popular welcome that went up for the visiting Americans.

That day in 2000 we rode into Cartagena as respected friends. President Clinton met with various groups and officials for the entire day and well into the evening. The sky was getting dark as we boarded the motorcade for the ride back to the airport.

Along the way, we were stunned to see that the Colombians who had welcomed us that morning were still there. They had waited along the road all day for this second fleeting glimpse of the Americans. Their enthusiasm was undiminished. I knew they were cheering for the president, but not just for the president. *This is how they feel about America. About Americans.*

I felt proud and humbled at the same time. We were a good country trying to do the right thing in the world, and we were respected in this foreign land.

The picture I keep in my head of our cheering Colombian friends will never fade. It comes flooding back vividly whenever I reflect on what has changed since then, how President George W. Bush, through word and deed, has strengthened our enemies and turned friends the world over against us. When President Bush went to Colombia seven years later, in March 2007, the government had to deploy twenty-eight thousand police and troops to keep order, and some anti-American demonstrators were tear-gassed.

Memorably, when Prime Minister Silvio Berlusconi of Italy addressed a joint session of Congress on March 1, 2006, he recalled the brief window of time between the end of the cold war and the start of this disastrous war in Iraq.

"In 2001, in the early days of my second government, I was called to chair the G-8 summit in Genoa," Berlusconi told the Congress. "After the conclusion of the summit's official program, the final dinner became a dinner among friends. . . . President Bush was chatting amiably with Prime Minister Junichiro Koizumi of Japan. Pearl Harbor and Hiroshima were but a distant memory. Prime Minister [Tony] Blair was joking with Chancellor [Gerhard] Schroeder. And the President of the Russian Federation, Vladimir Putin, was also talking with President Bush. The tragedy of the Second World War and the cold war, which had lasted for so many years, was forgotten. I felt great pleasure inside. I thought the world had in fact changed, and how different and peaceful was the world we were handing to our children. An age of lasting peace beckoned."

That was the world the Colombians were cheering on the road to Cartagena. As we touched down at Andrews Air Force

Base that night, I was excited to be part of this great moment in history, when "a lasting peace beckoned" and the world was looking to America for leadership. To help bring that about, I had to do my best on more mundane issues, certainly. The campaign back home was getting intense, and I wanted to be able to say I had voted, even in my brief tenure, to raise the minimum wage and to stop overtaxing married couples and people who inherit a small business. This was what my training and experience in Warwick had been all about: making things better at ground level, where people live.

It was a longstanding inequity in our income tax code that an unmarried couple filing separately pays less than a married couple filing jointly. We would have to draw down some of the federal budget surplus to pay for abolishing the "Marriage Penalty Tax," but what a good use for the surplus. I thought eliminating this inequity would honor the political sacrifices that Republican and Democratic presidents alike had made to end deficit spending in America. In the 1980s, when President Ronald Reagan recognized that his tax cuts were too deep, he went back and moderated them, and then paid a political price by losing seats in Congress. President George Herbert Walker Bush, whom I admire, jeopardized his chances for a second term when, for the good of the country, he went back on his unequivocal pledge: "Read my lips. No new taxes."

Finally, President Clinton had raised taxes to balance the budget, especially taxes on the wealthy. That more than anything else cost him both houses of Congress in 1994.

Now that we no longer had to spend enormous sums to counterbalance the former Soviet Union, it was time to do constructive things with our hard-won surplus. Both parties overwhelmingly supported fixing the marriage penalty and raising the modest $675,000 exemption on what is variously called the estate tax, the inheritance tax, or the death tax.

Americans who inherit assets worth $675,000 are not among the superrich. Both parties agree that Uncle Sam should not tax someone who inherits a small construction company that has a couple of bulldozers, backhoes, and dump trucks or someone whose parents owned valuable farmland but barely made a living on it.

We were all in a position to fix those injustices because we had the luxury of surpluses. On both taxes, however, our Republican majority went too far and sent bills to President Clinton that would have cut too deeply into the emerging surplus and put us back in the red.

Republicans who wanted to borrow money, spend it, and not worry about paying it back? That was a foreign concept to me.

The GOP leadership added billions in tax breaks for Republican constituencies. President Clinton vetoed these bills in the fall of 2000, at the height of the campaign season. In his veto message on the Death Tax Elimination Act of 2000, the president said, "This bill is fiscally irresponsible and provides a very expensive tax break for the best-off Americans while doing nothing for the vast majority of working families."

The Republican plan would "squander the surplus," he said.

President Clinton also vetoed the Marriage Tax Relief Reconciliation Act of 2000, calling it "poorly targeted and one part of a costly and regressive tax plan that reverses the principle of fiscal responsibility that has contributed to the longest economic expansion in history."

He was right, and most Republican senators agreed privately that he was right. But our election-year stance was that we were out there on the ramparts of freedom, gallantly fighting to keep Democrats from collecting taxes.

I parted ways with my leadership on these votes and supported Democratic amendments that targeted the relief where it was needed: the marriage penalty and the inheritance tax on middle-income people. That was better for America and good for the GOP politically, I argued. *We're in the majority. Let's pass a bill that President Clinton will sign and then remind the voters that it was our bill.*

As a rookie senator with just a year under my belt, I was worried that my challenger might sink my campaign by clobbering me with the Mike Brophy question: *Name just one thing you have accomplished.* Certainly, it was in my party's political interest for every Republican incumbent to be able to point with pride to a long-overdue increase in the minimum wage and a tax code we had made fairer for married couples, small business owners, and farmers. It was infuriating to me, as a struggling candidate, that the GOP leadership was against common sense.

President Clinton was leaving office. If he looked as good as we did on the minimum wage and tax fairness, so what? I saw no downside for anyone, least of all the working Americans we were in Washington to represent. And why would it be smart politically to hammer home the belief that only Democrats cared about the average American?

I was dismayed to see my Republican leadership turn an

easy call into an object lesson in *Why should everyone be allowed to win?*

The routine never changed: Republicans would pass a bill despite a veto threat, the president would exercise his veto, we would fail to override, and it all went into the paper recycling bin, with frustration all around. It was institutionalized gridlock. We did this pointless dance of death on many issues facing the Senate in 2000, large and small. If Republicans alone could not prevail by overturning a presidential veto, the leadership was determined to see neither party prevail.

I saw it as a destructive brand of politics, and a corruption of the high privilege we held as makers of public policy.

The leadership wanted us posturing for the 2000 election, polishing our credentials as True Republicans, getting airtime on talk radio as loyal soldiers who were out there landing punches against the enemy Liberals. That was somehow to be preferred over working with fellow Americans of whatever political stripe to get things done.

I parted company with the leadership on these tactics, as did a few other moderate Republicans. In his State of the Union address in January, President Clinton had telegraphed five issues that he thought would work to Democrats' advantage at election time: the minimum wage, a patients' bill of rights, campaign finance reform, gun safety, and an up-or-down vote on his judicial nominees. In February, I wrote to Majority Leader Trent Lott and proposed ideas on how to counter the Democratic offensive. At the time, Senator Lott and House Speaker Dennis Hastert were planning to assemble the Republican caucus at the Greenbrier Hotel, in the scenic mountains of West Virginia, just over the Virginia line, where we would talk about our agenda and how to win votes in November.

I cautioned the Senate majority leader on this absurd and fruitless routine we were doing with the Clinton White House. I said it would backfire on us as a party and that on election day we stood to "take a whipping like a Mississippi mule."

What Republican wants to go before the voters and boast of having obstructed an increase in the minimum wage?

Did we really want to be the party that said to ailing Americans, *We're with the big health maintenance organizations. Even if you have a legitimate grievance we're denying you the right to sue them.*

I told the majority leader I would have to skip the mountaintop retreat, I would be busy campaigning in Rhode Island and "working to do my part to keep a [Republican] majority."

If he gave more than a passing thought to the electoral dangers I foresaw, he never mentioned it. To be fair, I know he was hearing from other voices in the caucus, voices that were many times louder than mine. And I knew he was inclined to listen to them. After all, Republicans had won the Senate majority in 1994 by pushing this heavy right-wing agenda.

But times had changed. It was clear that voters were sick of seeing us accomplish nothing in Washington, and that had me worried about the future of my party. The Gingrich revolution and the sour rhetoric of talk radio had run its course. Voters wanted us to move beyond the get-Clinton era and start getting things done.

The majority leader did not respond to my letter. We would speak often about politics in the year ahead, but I could see he was determined to plow forward with the blinders on. In November, the voters spoke. They ousted five incumbents in the Republican caucus: Bill Roth of Delaware, chairman of the powerful Finance Committee, John Ashcroft of Missouri, Slade Gorton of Washington, Spencer Abraham of Michigan, and Rod Grams of Minnesota. All had played a leading role that year in achieving stalemate on President Clinton's legislative agenda. They were some of Trent Lott's most loyal bullfrogs.

The voters saw us as the party that wanted Americans to keep working for $5.15 an hour, that protected HMOs and the pharmaceutical industry.

At the same time, our presidential candidate, Texas governor George W. Bush, was in. He had run away from the caricature of a mean-spirited GOP. He had billed himself as "a compassionate conservative," a man of sound values who stood ready to use the tools of government to help the needy. His "humble foreign policy" would win new friends for America the world over, like those cheering Colombians on the road to Cartagena. And even though he had come out of the oil industry, he had played the right tune on the environment, pledging, at a campaign stop at Saginaw, Michigan, to regulate carbon dioxide emissions, thereby recognizing that greenhouse gas as a pollutant.

Governor Bush did not defend Republican meanness or the drive to impeach Clinton. He took the high road, and Americans gave him their vote while cleaning house in the Senate.

4

WINNING IN 2000

In November 2000, I won my race for the United States Senate over a formidable opponent, Democratic congressman Robert Weygand. Certainly, the year I had served as Governor Lincoln Almond's appointee was critical to my success. And there was a great outpouring of affection for my late father, which played a role in the outcome.

Congressman Weygand had warned voters that returning me to the Senate could be the margin that kept Republicans in power as the majority, controlling every committee chairmanship and the legislative agenda. But the overwhelmingly Democratic voters of Rhode Island did not buy the argument that ousting me would change the Senate. They could not be persuaded that Republican Senate control was in play, nor could the pundits.

Weygand was right. If one more incumbent Republican had gone down in flames, me or any other, Democrats would have had the majority. The new Senate was split down the middle, fifty Republicans to fifty Democrats.

Senator Ashcroft had served Missouri for twenty-four years as attorney general, governor, and U.S. senator, but voters were so fed up with stalemate and right-wing extremism they ousted him by throwing their support to a dead man. Democratic challenger Mel Carnahan died in a plane crash during the campaign, but his name remained on the ballot. When the late Mel Carnahan defeated Ashcroft, his widow, Jean Carnahan, was appointed to take his seat.

At the other end of the Republican spectrum, moderates Olympia Snowe of Maine, Jim Jeffords of Vermont, and I were returned to the Senate with strong margins. That meant something important, and we thought the leadership should take notice. We had bucked the Republican agenda on some bills and America apparently wanted more of it.

The race for president officially ended when Vice President Al Gore, in his role as Senate president, presided over the counting of the electoral ballots. I was in the House chamber as he officiated over the process that ended his exhausting quest for the presidency in 2000. The vice president showed good humor and grace in performing the task the Constitution assigned to him. It was his duty to preside over his own defeat, and I thought he discharged it well in the most trying personal circumstances.

I was in the chamber as a Republican to ensure that the process would go as the Constitution prescribed and that my party would come out of it with control of the White House. Despite that illusion-shattering lunch with Vice President-elect Cheney and all that was said there, I still had the desire and hope that President-elect Bush's deeds would match his campaign rhetoric. He might yet live up to his solemn promise to America and govern as a uniter, not a divider.

Members of the Congressional Black Caucus stood that day and asked if even one member of the Senate would speak up and contest the election results. Under the Constitution, that is all it takes, one voice calling the result into doubt. The men and women of the Black Caucus implored us to reject the inevitability of a President George W. Bush. Their pleas seemed more than merely political; I saw in them a genuine fear of what might lie ahead if Governor Bush were elevated to the presidency.

Of course, if we senators had known then how far this new administration would go to undercut the Congress—to wage war wherever it pleases, for however long, at whatever cost—I think many of my colleagues would have answered the pleas of the Black Caucus that day.

I know I would have.

The members of that caucus were simply more attuned than the rest of us to picking up the danger signals coming from the extreme right, perhaps because the right had incited such ugly racial suspicions and even hatred in winning the Republican South Carolina primary for Bush.

Bush supporters ruthlessly defamed Senator John McCain in South Carolina. McCain had won the New Hampshire primary and had to be destroyed. No tactic was too obscene to dissuade the Bush operatives in South Carolina, who, oddly enough, think of themselves as the most virtuous people in America. Utterly convinced that their cause is right, they allowed themselves to do anything to win.

The South Carolina primary is known as the Lee Atwater firewall, after the late GOP operative. Right-wing Republicans never liked to see New Hampshire allowed to establish momentum for their party's presidential nominee. New Hampshire, after all, is in New England and therefore suspect. They threw the firewall up, and it worked to shameful perfection. It stopped McCain's momentum dead and put George Bush on the road to the Republican nomination.

The extremists backing Bush made anonymous accusations on talk radio. They printed fliers aimed at inciting ignorance and racism and left them on windshields in church parking lots. They used family photos of Senator and Mrs. McCain and their adopted child from Bangladesh to accuse McCain of going outside his marriage for interracial sex. At the same time, candidate Bush was appearing before adoring crowds at Bob Jones University, where interracial dating was forbidden.

The tactics that Bush supporters used against Senator McCain in South Carolina were beyond imagination and played to the voters' worst instincts. In the thrill of winning, many Republicans forgot about the means employed to that end, but they were not so easily forgotten by the Black Caucus.

When Vice President Gore abandoned his run for the presidency and conceded defeat, the Republican caucus was ready to set its agenda for the 107th Congress. As we assembled in the Library of Congress, one of the most magnificent buildings on Capitol Hill, Senate Republicans were still shaking their heads in disbelief that voters had unseated five of their incumbent colleagues. Four of the losses came in critical swing states, Michigan, Washington, Minnesota, and Missouri. To the voters, it was not about control of the Senate; it was about punishing the most vocal supporters of an extremist agenda that middle America did not endorse. The fact that Jim Jeffords and I could win in overwhelmingly Democratic states sent a message to the leadership, but one they refused to hear.

Given our deep losses in the Senate, some Republicans wanted to throw out the day's agenda and talk about what had gone wrong. But most insisted on plowing ahead without discussion or reflection. The lessons of November 2000 were unimportant. Why? Because William Jefferson Clinton of Arkansas had vetoed his last Republican bill.

We had the White House now. We had the House of Representatives as well, and the 50–50 Senate was 51–50 in practice, given that the vice president would be on hand to break every tie vote in our favor.

Our leadership gleefully looked ahead to at least two years of steamroller Republican rule in America. If the voters who had sacked our powerful incumbents were trying to send us a message, it was old news. Our caucus leadership was focused on the hard-core conservative mission before us: to push through unprecedented tax cuts, weaken environmental regulations, and starve social programs. Because of a decision made by our retreat leader, Senator Kay Bailey Hutchison of Texas, there was no escaping the message that Republicans preferred to ignore that day. Senator Hutchison had arranged for pollster John Zogby of Zogby International to address us at the Library of Congress on the mood of the country.

Mr. Zogby's research explained concisely why the voters had returned me, Olympia Snowe, and Jim Jeffords, but had retired senators Ashcroft, Roth, Abraham, Gorton, and Grams.

He said voters wanted both parties "to reconnect with the vital center" and "focus less attention on the intense core voters." They were unhappy that Republicans had spent so much time stoking the passions of the base and inciting pointless division in the Clinton years. By 2000, voters were fed up with the Republican Revolution of 1994 led by House Speaker Newt Gingrich. They did not want a legislative stalemate driven by political extremism of any kind, right or left.

"I want you to be assured that none of these remarks are tailored in any way," Mr. Zogby told us. "I would give this exact speech to the Democratic Conference.

"In the broad scope of things, there were no real winners on November 7 or its aftermath," he said. "In many respects, both presidential candidates lost this election. It was a tie. There was neither a conservative nor a liberal mandate. There was no resounding victory on a national level anywhere to be seen.

"Your core voters on the Right are very intense, but you are going to have to explain this new reality to them. You will have to tell them that there is a Democratic Party, it is not evil incarnate, and that its candidates for Congress and President got as many votes as you did. Explain to them that they are not going away and that the voters have expressed a desire for a national vision that is bipartisan."

That was a fact that George Bush had apprehended on his own, judging by his campaign rhetoric that year, those reassuring promises of a unifying agenda and a "humble foreign policy." That approach had won him votes from many of the same Americans who were telling John Zogby they were fed up with extremism.

Here at the Library of Congress we were setting an agenda for the next two years, fresh on the heels of accepting, as our president, a candidate who received fewer votes than his opponent, and had been awarded the presidency by a five-to-four vote in the Supreme Court. Now our own pollster was telling us we had to reconnect to the vital center to avoid repeating the kind of losses we had just suffered in the Senate. In the next several hours we resolved to do exactly the opposite.

The ideologues prevailed at the Library of Congress and again when we elected our leadership team for the 107th Congress. Without opposition, Senator Trent Lott was back in as majority leader; without opposition, Don Nickels of Oklahoma, back in as whip; without opposition, Kay Bailey Hutchison, conference secretary; without opposition, Bill Frist of Tennessee, chairman of the Republican Senatorial Committee. Senator Rick Santorum of Pennsylvania easily had the votes for conference chairman. The only truly contested race was for chairman of our policy committee. Given that we had just seen five Republican incumbents go down in defeat, I argued that a little ideological diversity in the leadership would do us good. The closest thing to that would be Senator Pete Domenici of New Mexico winning the policy chairmanship over the far-right senator Larry Craig of Idaho. Many Republicans thought that was a good idea, but when the secret ballots were counted, Larry Craig had twenty-six votes to Pete Domenici's twenty-four. Nothing was going to change. In the 107th Congress Republicans would speak with the same monolithic voice of old. I was surprised that no one in the leadership saw the danger in that. In any organization, it makes sense to hear different viewpoints, and Pete Domenici might have brought that much-needed bit of change. Instead, we would have a bloc of hard-right voices dominating the leadership over the next two years, and worse, the public face of the leadership.

5

THE STALKING HORSE

On Inauguration Day, January 20, 2001, the Bush-Cheney team went to work on the real agenda. The president wasted no time in taking on the most divisive and emotional issue in America: abortion. As one of his first official acts, he rescinded a Clinton executive order that had allowed foreign nongovernmental organizations to provide abortion services and still receive U.S. aid. That was a powerful symbolic move, certainly not done thoughtlessly. The president was sending a message to the base, the people who had pulled out all the stops for him in South Carolina: *We're in power now.*

The agenda that Cheney had dropped on us in Senator Specter's hideaway office was quickly becoming reality. Its centerpiece was an unprecedented $1.6 trillion tax cut. The magnitude of the cut caught even House Speaker Dennis Hastert by surprise. That may have accounted for his candor, at a December 14, 2000, press conference, when he said that an across-the-board cut of historic proportions was too much; it would be bad public policy. No one would be able to fully understand the consequences of such a complex bill. He wanted to break the cuts down into their many parts and carefully consider one at a time. He was quickly silenced and brought into line. This was the first big fight the president sparked in the Congress. After presidents of both parties had worked hard for surpluses, and at dire political cost, why was the forty-third president now demanding this destructive round of tax cuts?

Many senators in the chamber had been around in the 1980s when so much effort went into the Gramm-Rudman deficit reductions. Finance chairman Charles Grassley of Iowa and Budget chairman Pete Domenici were among them. Many were there in 1990 when the president's father, President George H. W. Bush, agreed to raise taxes to shrink the deficit, a big factor in his loss two years later.

With presidential leadership exercised and political pain already endured, why would we suddenly want to turn the Treasury upside down and shake out every last dime?

To me, the tax cut was a stalking horse. The Cheney-Bush strategy behind the cut was to set the tone—to preempt the Congress not just on taxes but on every issue. It would tame any future resistance to a radical agenda by serving up this politically irresistible prize: Lawmakers could go home and say they had voted to cut taxes. The White House was out to neuter Congress, and the minute Congress rolled over for the cuts, it set the stage for one-branch rule in America and all the consequences we live with today. The two aggressive personalities at the top of the executive branch had tested the Congress and had found it lacking. *A coequal branch of government?* In their wisdom, the Founders had given us power to respond when events demand that we check and balance an unwise president. I looked around in the Senate and saw few who had the courage to wield that vital power.

Every bully and blowhard in the world sets the terms of intimidation right off the bat. The time to stand up is sooner instead of later. My older brother, Zech, taught me that important lesson by example when I was in the third grade at Potowomut Elementary School. In front of a cheering schoolyard, he put up his fists and boxed a bully out of a bad attitude. But the president had our number the minute we meekly acquiesced to his radical tax policy, and that would serve him well when he wanted to start a war on the false threat of a Saddam Hussein poised to attack America with weapons of mass destruction.

For many Americans, their first real memory of the Bush presidency is date-stamped September 11, 2001. They forget the pitched political battles of his first nine months in office. The central front in his war on Congress was this $1.6 trillion raid on the public purse.

The outcome was uncertain given the dynamics of an evenly divided Senate. Democrats were largely opposed, but Georgia Democrat Zell Miller, a throwback to the pre–civil rights South, had defected and even signed on as a cosponsor of the Bush tax cuts. Democrats were especially worried that John Breaux of Louisiana and Ben Nelson of Nebraska might waver. The Bush administration certainly put every bit of pressure they could on senators Breaux and Nelson back home, and on every other Democrat in a state that had voted Bush-Cheney.

The Democrats held steady, and in April, Ben Nelson, John Breaux, and I called a press conference to say we would use our votes to trim the $1.6 trillion to $1.25 trillion. If we could get one more Republican to stand with us, we could make it happen. We needed Jim Jeffords of Vermont and had been told to expect him at the press conference, but where was he? Stalling for time, Senator Breaux cracked jokes to keep an impatient media at least semi-entertained. Then the blue curtains at the edge of the Capitol press gallery parted and in walked the Vermonter, our critical vote.

This was historic. Two Republicans and two Democrats had teamed up to deal a symbolic defeat to the Cheney-Bush team. It may seem ridiculous to call a $350 billion "trim" merely symbolic, but it was, in the context of the monstrous $1.6 trillion the White House demanded. But the administration insisted on getting it all. To them, a penny less would mean total defeat. Their thinking, I concluded, was that any reduction, no matter how small, would telegraph that Congress had a role to play in governing America, and the executive branch was something less than all-powerful.

That was the important point we four rebels meant to drive home, and the administration knew it. Once we had the clout to trim the president's $1.6 trillion, we used it. A preliminary budget vote related to the bill went according to form, with Democrat Miller defecting, Breaux, Nelson, and the rest of the Democrats holding, Jeffords and I voting in favor from the Republican side, bolstered by unexpected last-minute support from Republican Arlen Specter.

The administration had really cranked up the pressure on the vote to enact the bill, even calling local talk radio to do some arm-twisting. My turn came on the *Steve Kass Show,* a middle-of-the-road program with no particular ideological bent, broadcast from a modest studio on Wampanoag Trail in East Providence, Rhode Island. One morning the phone rang and instead of Angelo from Cranston it was Vice President Richard Cheney from Washington. He hit all the radical talking points and urged Rhode Islanders to demand that I vote to return their unspent tax dollars to them and keep not a penny in reserve. It would be the end of all that was good if I supported a cut of $1.5999999999 trillion. The president needed the $1.6.

The administration did some arm-twisting up close and personal as well. One day, in the Senate chamber, a White House liaison tapped me on the shoulder. *The vice president wants to see you.*

I knew it was about the tax cut. I welcomed the chance to discuss my opposition face-to-face and was curious to see how the vice president would counter the points I made. As a former mayor and city councilman, I know about taxes. Eight times in my career I stood for election in campaigns where taxes were at least a leading issue and sometimes *the* issue. I had something to say about taxes, and to say to the vice president in particular. If we were going to cut into the surplus that the president's father had helped achieve at enormous political cost, let us invest in our assets, as any smart business owner would. We could put people to work fixing our aging highways, bridges, and levees; fix the marriage penalty and the inheritance tax; start helping local governments with the crushing cost of meeting special-education mandates, and fund programs to put us on the path to energy and environmental sustainability.

Because there is always room for compromise, I wanted to discuss supporting some of the tax breaks the president wanted. We could never agree on all $1.6 trillion, but I was prepared to agree on some of it.

As the Senate's presiding officer, Vice President Cheney had an ornate office off the Senate floor. I was ushered in past the velvet ropes, took my seat, and soon realized that my opinions were not up for discussion. The vice president had called me in so he could explain why I had to vote for the $1.6 trillion as-is, why not a word was subject to amendment. It was a top-down, one-way "exchange of ideas," so to speak. His monologue went on for fifteen to twenty minutes. My thoughts on tax policy were unworthy of his time. I was furious. One side of me wanted to forget that I respected the office he held and talk to him as if we were a couple of blacksmiths in Alberta with a bad bet to settle, but I checked my temper, shook his hand, thanked him for having me in, and walked out.

I left the vice president's office even more firmly committed to resisting the president's tax policy.

No doubt this was just one of many I-talk-you-listen meetings the vice president held with senators and representatives. He must have certainly leaned hard on Speaker Hastert and House finance chairman Grassley after they told reporters they doubted the wisdom of a single up-or-down vote on the mega tax break.

"We are most successful, especially in tax policy, when we start to take tax ideas and do them a piece at a time," Hastert said. Grassley, too, called for taking it one step at a time, especially in a Senate equally divided. But the far right wing was rabid about "starving the beast," cutting taxes so deeply it would bring back deficits and force deep cuts in social spending, programs they saw as inevitably building Democratic constituencies. Instead of pushing back against the administration's ferocious demands on its radical agenda, leaders found it easier to fall in line. And this was the critical time for pushing back, the spring of 2001; Americans were not dying yet in the president's nation-building projects in Southwest Asia.

Zogby International had the data on how disgusted voters were with the extremist agenda, and yet here we were ramming through an extreme tax cut. Few Americans paid close attention to this pre-September 11 struggle in Congress, but the president was going back on many of his central campaign pledges, and Congress was boiling, no middle ground, no compromise. The tax cut was the main fight, but the environment and women's reproductive freedoms were in play, too.

The defection of Republican senator Jim Jeffords was a window into this early discord between the Congress and the new administration. He grasped fully the implications of the Bush-Cheney team embarking on its radical agenda and attempting to marginalize and undermine Congress.

Senator Jeffords had served in Washington for decades. In 1974 he was one of the few Republicans able to win election to the House in the immediate fallout of the Watergate scandal. He had seen a lot of ups and downs in the party's fortunes, but what was happening in Washington in the spring of 2001 led him to cross the aisle, become an independent and caucus with the Democrats.

Such defections are rare in the Senate, but they do happen.

In 1994, Democrat Richard Shelby of Alabama switched to the GOP side. Democrat Ben Nighthorse Campbell of Colorado did the same a few months later. But Jim Jeffords of Vermont is the only senator in history to alter control of the Senate between elections by doing so, unseating every committee chairman simply by crossing the aisle. He had dealt an enormous defeat to President Bush, and that took courage.

The Jeffords defection was a stark demonstration of how much turmoil the administration had caused with its assault on the Congress. The legislative branch was wracked with tension in the first eight months of 2001. That was why it took us until the Saturday before Memorial Day to adopt a budget, something normally done in March or April.

The Senate passed $1.25 trillion in cuts and the House had swallowed whole the president's demand for $1.6 trillion. The two bills were reconciled in a bitterly partisan conference. We finally called the roll on a $1.35 trillion "compromise." It was an absurd piece of legislation based on a budget gimmick.

Republican backers of the administration saved face by building in a ten-year sunset provision that, through some accounting sleight of hand, would allow them to claim they had gotten the full $1.6 trillion.

It was irresponsible lawmaking, and it created nightmares for financial planners that continue to this day. If you die on December 31, 2010, your heirs pay no estate tax; die a day later and they owe Uncle Sam 55 percent of everything beyond the first $675,000 of the estate, which is exempt.

Under the sunset provision in the new law, all the changes made in the spring of 2001 expire ten years later. Your heirs may owe astronomical taxes or no taxes at all, depending on when you "plan" to die. More than a few financial advisers have been met with uncomprehending stares when they explain the reality of this ludicrous law to a client.

No one knew when the conference committee would report out and we would be called in to vote on the Bush-Cheney tax cut. It came on a Saturday morning when everyone was scrambling to get home for the weeklong Memorial Day recess. I was in the Capitol that day, in casual clothes, and quickly borrowed a jacket, a tie, and a pair of dress shoes so I could be admitted to the chamber to cast my nay vote. For a moment I wondered if the tax cutters might be right and I might be wrong. Maybe we really could afford these tantalizing tax cuts.

Deep down, the fiscal conservative in me said, no, the sunset provisions are irresponsible. *Stick to your guns.*

Senator Jeffords, the man who turned over control of the Senate to the Democrats, strangely voted yea. It was a token peace offering and a parting gift to the Republican establishment that he had served for so many years. I had walked into the chamber thinking I would be the only Republican to vote against the tax cuts. To my surprise and delight, Senator John McCain had also voted nay. A legislative assistant called out the news to me as I closed the door to my office and headed home to Rhode Island for the recess. It certainly felt good to have some Republican company on this tough vote. Since John had not supported previous efforts to scale back the tax cut, I assumed he saw, as I did, the idiocy and irresponsibility of the sunset provision added in at the conference.

Nonetheless, Republicans back home were furious with me, despite their admiration for John McCain.

A few weeks later, I asked for a meeting with the president. I admired his father, President George H. W. Bush, and had gone to school with his brother, Jeb, then governor of Florida, but the president and I were not on familiar terms. We had shaken hands once or twice. Now he was the president, and I did not want any ill feelings to fester over the tax cut. I had done something like this several times before: After fighting with the Democrats on the Warwick City Council, I made a point of sitting down with them over a few beers at Saccoccio's. I wanted to tell the president I felt strongly that Democrats and Republicans needed to work together and needed his leadership to bring that about. He had promised as much during the campaign, and now we had a divisive fight over taxes, a Republican defection, and the Democrats were back in control of the Senate. But on another level, I just wanted to spend some valuable time with the president so I could get a sense of the person with whom I would share the reins of government for the next three and a half years.

The president welcomed me into the Oval Office. It was only my second time in that famous setting, the seat of executive authority in America. The president was friendly at first, but soon we were both being frank and I told him he was risking Republican seats in the Senate in 2002 with his hard-line agenda. We could lose moderates Susan Collins of Maine and Gordon Smith of Oregon. Their constituents would naturally associate them, as Republicans, with an extreme agenda and that would leave them vulnerable. "Don't worry about Susan and Gordon," he told me, in a tone that did not encourage further discussion of how his agenda might threaten us moderates. I asked why he was pushing a hard line on abortion when most Americans are sick of politicians stoking that emotional and most personal issue all the time. "Even Laura is pro-choice," I said, not knowing if it was true. I had read it somewhere and thought I could discern the truth in his reaction.

"Don't you bring my wife into this," the president snapped.

He did not deny that the first lady, like most American women, thinks the government should stay out of their most private and difficult moral decisions.

When the meeting ended, I felt worse about him than when I arrived. I was shaken. I admire old-fashioned virtues, chief among them, honesty. Even at this early date in his tenure, the president had demonstrated an undeniable capacity for mendacity. America took him at his word when he said he was a uniter, not a divider; that our foreign policy would be humble; that he would address climate change by regulating carbon dioxide. In the first months of his administration he had already turned his back on these bedrock campaign pledges.

My visit with the new president did nothing to assuage my apprehensions. The man, and by that I mean the inner man, the essential man, seemed unequal to the awesome powers entrusted to him. I was worried about the damage he might do over the next few years, never mind in a second term, which seemed unthinkable at the time.

What motivates a man to break his promises? I cannot help but think back to *A Charge to Keep,* the autobiography the Texas governor wrote in 1999, with his political communications director, Karen Hughes. I identify with a part of the book because the president and I have one sad event in common: we both lost a younger sister to an early death.

When I was fifteen, my sister, Tribbie, a gifted young horsewoman, died in a riding accident. I was away at school and learned of the tragedy in a television news report.

When President Bush was seven, he lost his sister, Robin, to leukemia.

When I read what he wrote about that experience, I thought I saw some deep scars there. One day his sister was gone and "no one talked about it much."

"The 1950s were a time when a death or any other personal tragedy in a family was viewed as just that: personal. I didn't know that, of course, I was only seven . . . I was young enough, and my parents loved me enough, that Robin's death did not traumatize me."

I felt bad when I read the president's account of an experience he had later, at boarding school, in writing a paper. "It was a story about emotions and I was trying to find a unique way to describe 'tears' running down my face. . . . The paper came back with a 'zero' marked so emphatically that it left an impression visible all the way through to the back of the blue book." How tragic that his teacher could not understand an obvious cry of anguish.

I intend no second-guessing of how the Bush family handled Robin's death. In such tragedies, every parent does their absolute best and deserves complete empathy and understanding. But I was so rattled by the president's words in the Oval Office I was casting about for clues as to how one man could be so ready to battle the world around him, on issues large and small.

Oddly, his pugnacious and intractable attitude remains a big part of his mystique with the Republican core that is still energized as I write this in 2007. Despite his many hollow words and the myriad failures—from Hurricane Katrina to Iraq to peace in the Middle East—the core still loves that President Bush will never back down or change course or admit error. Theirs is the rigid form of thinking that will define the smaller, more aggressive, more extreme Republican Party of the future.

AFTER THE MEMORIAL day recess, we came back and spent a sweltering summer rearranging chairs as the committees reorganized under Democratic leadership and the staffs changed accordingly. We did nothing on the issues important to voters.

That August, I picked up a *Bangor Daily News* while in Maine and read that the Bush-Cheney tax cuts were already proving too deep and that nonpartisan budget analysts were forecasting deficits. I thought this would have the Democrats, in their new majority, sharpening the long knives and spoiling for an even bloodier fight when we reconvened in September.

Of course, no one had any idea how dramatically the world would change that September. But even back in June, before we knew the president would soon lead our response to the murder of nearly three thousand American civilians, something very disturbing came through for me in his demeanor and attitude in the Oval Office. I want to describe it as insecurity, but even that is not the right word.

Several times, the president went out of his way to remind me that he was the commander in chief. *You don't have to keep telling me that,* I thought. *I know who you are.* Like others, I have been around people who are good at wielding power. They never have to tell you they are in charge. They just *are,* and you know it. What I saw and heard that day really unsettled me. *I'm the commander in chief . . . I'm the president . . . I'm the commander in chief . . .* It was unpresidential.

That September, as I watched the Twin Towers collapse in smoke and dust, I had a sinking feeling about the president's capacity to respond wisely.

6

AL-QAEDA STRIKES

On September 11, 2001, I drove into Washington under a clear blue sky, one of those beautiful mornings you remember. Within an hour, of course, the day became memorable not for its beauty but its horror.

In my office in the Russell Building, my scheduler, Betty Dudik, and I stood and watched a television image of the World Trade Center burning. Then, at 9:03, United Airlines Flight 175 crashed into the second tower and the nation suddenly knew that a coordinated attack against us was under way. When American Airlines Flight 77 hit the Pentagon, about three miles away, security officials started evacuating our building.

Once outside there was a tremendous noise that no one could pinpoint and I heard somebody say, *They've bombed the State Department.* This was not the case, we would learn later. Some thought we had heard a scrambled warplane breaking the sound barrier, but I never did hear any authoritative word on the cause.

Lawmakers and staff simply went to their cars and left the city. There was no plan in place for where the Senate should reconvene in an emergency, not even in the event of a natural disaster, let alone an attack by a foreign enemy. We simply filtered away from Capitol Hill.

The next day I made a statement on the Senate floor, as many did.

"I support the president's efforts to marshal the resources of our intelligence, law enforcement, diplomatic and military apparatus to bring about justice and to do so as swiftly as possible," I said. "I believe people around the world are in equal measure demanding justice for these horrendous crimes and anxious for a world that can settle its disputes in a rational, civilized manner. We must cling to the hope that this is possible, even while we recognize that on this earth exist people capable of unbelievable barbarity."

Then I asked my staff to get me everything they could find on Osama bin Laden, the Saudi identified in news reports as the suspected mastermind behind the attacks.

I had heard of the Palestinian Abu Nidal and other notorious terrorists operating around the world, but never bin Laden. I was in the Senate when the USS *Cole* was bombed off the coast of Yemen; to my recollection, the high-level intelligence briefings we received afterward never focused on bin Laden. Within hours, my staff handed over a great deal of information about the Saudi founder of the al-Qaeda terror network. I was particularly interested to learn that John Miller of ABC News had interviewed bin Laden in southern Afghanistan in May 1998. I wanted to know what motivated this sort of murderous fury unleashed against civilians.

It was not a popular question to ask, given that many leaders in Washington were stoking emotions and even rage instead of seeking to calm the public, get the facts, and strike appropriately at this enemy. They just wanted to kill somebody back—*now*.

I was for heeding Sun-tzu, who wrote, in *The Art of War:* "Thus it is said that one who knows the enemy and knows himself will not be endangered in a hundred engagements. One who does not know the enemy, but knows himself, will sometimes be victorious, sometimes meet with defeat. One who knows neither the enemy nor himself will invariably be defeated in every engagement."

Those of us who wanted to know the enemy in 2001 were denounced by the braying conservative talking heads as appeasers, akin to Neville Chamberlain. To the contrary, Chamberlain's appeasement of Adolf Hitler supported our very point: He had failed to know his enemy.

At this writing, President Bush often points to the words of Osama bin Laden as proof that we need to wage endless war in Iraq, but in September 2001 those of us who wanted to know what drove bin Laden's rage against us were looked upon with suspicion.

Bin Laden had talked extensively about three grievances: American military bases near the holy sites of Mecca and Medina, in his native Saudi Arabia; the plight of the Palestinians under Israeli occupation in Gaza and the West Bank; and the misery of the Iraqi people living under U.N. sanctions.

As I read the materials my staff gathered, I felt we had to define two missions ahead: to pursue bin Laden with every ounce of vigor and bring him to justice, and to deny future bin Ladens the propaganda tools that had recruited the nineteen men who brought down our airliners in New York, Virginia, and Pennsylvania.

That seemed a methodical way to retaliate for the September 11 attacks and minimize the likelihood of future, perhaps even more devastating, attacks.

Two days later, on Friday, September 14, Congress met to empower the president to use military power against the al-Qaeda terrorist network. Befitting our divided, polarized government, Democrats met in one room, Republicans in another, to read the same hastily drafted resolution authorizing the president to take us to war. All we had in front of us was a one-page war authorization marked across the top DRAFT—DRAFT—DRAFT—DRAFT. This unofficial document described the attacks against us as "treacherous." Someone had crossed out "treacherous" and penciled in "despicable."

Washington was in such a panic we were going to unleash the might of the world's only and greatest superpower with a draft document scribbled on by an unknown hand. There was no time for an intern to push a button on a copier and run off a hundred clean copies of an official resolution sending American men and women to fight and die in Southwest Asia. As we filed into the chamber to vote, I said to Senator Gordon Smith of Oregon, "We have to slow this thing down. We haven't thought this through. We haven't had any real discussion." He turned to me and said, "The train has left the station, Linc."

He could not have been more right. The rush to war had the mass and inertia of a 534-car freight train. The Republican leadership wanted two immediate and unanimous votes. A few senior senators would be allowed to read statements but there would be no debate on the two issues before us: sending emergency aid to New York and unleashing President Bush on our enemies. I upset that plan—at least the desired unanimity—when I voted no on the first roll the parliamentarians called. Jaws dropped. My colleagues said, *You're voting against the money for New York?* I said, *No, I'm voting against going to war in the next ten minutes. We need to discuss this first.*

Events played out chaotically from there. I certainly wanted to send emergency funds to New York City, so I hustled down to the well of the Senate and asked the parliamentarians to verify the question pending on the floor. I said I wanted to vote nay on the rush to war and yea on the funding. Even the parliamentarians could not tell me which vote they were calling first and which would be second. They were disputing that very issue among themselves *while calling the roll!* But that was how it went that day: Senators voted to authorize war thinking they were sending emergency aid to New York City; they voted to aid New York thinking they were authorizing war. Before the roll call had been completed, having been implored by my staff to reconsider, I did change my vote and in the end I voted yea on both. If nothing else, it saved us from having to get my long-suffering chief of staff, David Griswold, up off the floor with cardiac paddles. Had I voted no, David would have spent every waking hour dealing with the political backlash against me. Out of 535 members in both houses of Congress, Representative Barbara Lee of Oakland, California, would be the only one to vote nay on the Afghanistan war authorization. She was the one missing car in the freight train. She received numerous death threats and a Capitol Police security detail was assigned to protect her around the clock.

On September 16, the president announced, in the Rose Garden, of all places, that "this crusade, this war on terrorism, is going to take awhile." This was provocative language that played into the hands of our enemies. Osama bin Laden had denounced Americans as "crusaders" when rallying his followers to attack us.

Four days later, on September 20, President Bush addressed a joint session of Congress in the House chamber. I was seated on the far edge, next to a group of foreign diplomats.

The president used the words "terror" or "terrorists" thirty-three times in a thirty-four-minute speech. He said we were suddenly swept up in history and enlisted in "a great cause." We would hunt down "the enemies of freedom," for "freedom itself is under attack." The terrorists were "traitors to their own faith" and had attempted "to hijack Islam itself" in a drive to "plot evil and destruction."

President Bush was in his element. He incited passions with bombast, sentiment, and the smirking melodrama of his own personal preparedness for battle. *I will not forget this wound . . . I will not yield, I will not rest, I will not relent . . .* A chamber filled with fear and bravado responded with thirty ovations and shouts of encouragement.

Interestingly, there was one section of his speech where there was no applause; it was when he attempted to describe and define the al-Qaeda enemy and its goals. "Americans have many questions tonight. Americans are asking: Who attacked our country?" He spoke of "a person named Osama bin Laden" who practiced "a fringe form of Islamic extremism."

This was the "great cause" of the new century? To wage world war against a "fringe" group of Islamic cutthroats?

I felt differently. We needed to find and destroy this small band of international criminals, disarm their propaganda machine, and use hard-nosed police work to prevent future attacks. It was paramount to remain focused on the truly great cause of our time, to provide American leadership to the world in an age of unparalleled promise. That day was upon us. Silvio Berlusconi would memorably describe it in this very chamber, speaking of "how different and peaceful was the world we were handing to our children." When "an age of lasting peace beckoned," the president exhorted us to abandon the fruits of our cold war victory and organize our world around yet another global conflict, this time with no apparent end.

He would take us into "a lengthy campaign, unlike any other we have ever seen."

A traumatized people need to hear calming language from their leaders. Instead, the president poured fuel onto the emotions of the moment in his address to Congress. He dialed in the fear.

"I ask you to live your lives and hug your children. I know many citizens have fears tonight, and I ask you to be calm and resolute, even in the face of a continuing threat."

He paid lip service to the need for calm while issuing threats and inciting the national grief and rage with slogans.

"Every nation in every region now has a decision to make, either you are with us or you are with the terrorists," he said. "Americans are asking, why do they hate us? . . . They hate our freedoms. Our freedom of religion, our freedom of speech, our freedom to vote and assemble and disagree with each other."

He had not invested ten seconds in the central admonition of Sun-tzu: *Know your enemy.* He said not a word to address the presence of American troops near Mecca and Medina, or the Palestinian question, or sanctions against Iraq. Not a word about how we were going to deny bin Laden his propaganda victories on these issues, and his well-used recruitment tools.

President Bush thanked the Congress for its leadership on September 11, which he defined as singing a patriotic song. In reality, most members had abandoned their oaths of office and yielded all leadership responsibility to the White House.

"I thank the Congress for its leadership at such an important time. All of America was touched on the evening of the tragedy to see Republicans and Democrats joined together on the steps of this Capitol, singing 'God Bless America.' "

I looked at my fellow members of Congress to my left and the diplomats on my right and wondered if anyone else in the chamber was as unmoved by the Bush fervor as I.

To my right were eight or ten ambassadors from nations in Africa, in colorful, traditional dress. They were the only faces I could see that appeared unnerved by the president's belligerent tone in this foreboding moment in American history.

The president ended his address to the joint session of Congress that mild September night by pledging that we would "meet violence with patient justice assured of the rightness of our cause and confident of the victories to come in all that lies before us, may God grant us wisdom and may He watch over the United States of America."

Wisdom, of course, would be the key to our success in fighting al-Qaeda, but the president said nothing that evening to show he had the capacity to effectively combat the anger and hatred that were behind these diabolical attacks.

As the chamber erupted in sustained applause, I looked to my left at my fellow members of Congress and saw that everyone was caught up in the moment. It reminded me of the Confederate jubilation at Twelve Oaks, the Wilkes plantation in *Gone with the Wind,* when the barbeque is interrupted by news that a glorious war has been declared. Both sides were quickly disillusioned when the ghastly carnage was upon them. We should never cheer the outbreak of war; war is the failure of everything for which we should strive. While senators cheered loudly, I had a flicker of kinship instead with the foreign ambassadors on my right. There I saw a muted reaction. They seemed to sense, perhaps from their own experience on a war-plagued continent, that a hasty and ill-defined rush to arms can bring horrific and unforeseen consequences.

The architects of the president's performance had orchestrated a moment of genius. They had everything they wanted—a traumatized nation, an adoring Congress—and they skillfully brought out the props on cue. In the first forty-five seconds, the president introduced Lisa Beamer, the bereaved widow of Todd Beamer, one of the brave passengers who, with an inspiring "Let's roll," fought the hijackers of United Airlines Flight 93 over Pennsylvania. Then he trotted out Tony Blair. "America has no truer friend than Great Britain. Once again we are joined together in a great cause—so honored the British prime minister has crossed an ocean to show his unity of purpose with America." Then, since every moment of crisis needs an unveiling, the president announced that he had formed an Office of Homeland Security. His new assistant to the president for Homeland Security was Republican governor Tom Ridge of Pennsylvania, who waved on cue. Acknowledged also were New York governor George Pataki and Mayor Rudy Giuliani, the New Yorkers who did indeed step into leadership roles on September 11. There was long, long applause, as their on-the-street experience that dark day was transferred to the commander in chief, who had spent the day in safety, far from the attacks. And the president ended his display of props by telling the nation that he would always carry the police shield of a man named George Howard, who died trying to save others in the World Trade Center. More transferred heroism, transferred by the talisman of a badge. I was not buying it, even if our political institutions and news media were. If the president could not be counted on to keep faith with his campaign promises, how could he be trusted with a challenge that demanded the wisest president in a century? Even the wisest president ever?

To me, he was the same man who had seemed so insecure in the Oval Office just three months before, and I simply had no faith in his temperament or his ability to tell the truth.

I continued to express, to every reporter who asked, that I thought our response should be a dual track: Go after the men behind September 11 with every ounce of energy, and come to grips with the issues that they exploited to motivate a motley group to perform a highly coordinated and complex mission. The hijackers had lived among us for two years, never getting caught, never at risk of being exposed through the defection of one of their own. We needed to understand that drive if we intended to succeed in preventing similar attacks.

The mood across the country and in Rhode Island, especially among Republicans on talk radio, was extremely critical that I would even hint at a strategic need to understand what motivated our enemies. They were focused on tactics, giving the president power to pursue and identify enemies wherever they might be and dispatch them as quickly as possible.

When the address to the joint session ended, Majority Leader Tom Daschle embraced the president. The footage of that hug would play a role in Daschle's defeat in his 2004 re-election campaign. The embrace, though at the president's initiative, came across as an abject plea from a weak Congress for the commander in chief to save us from our foes. It was embarrassing in its symbolism. The emasculation that the tax cut had started was made complete by September 11. The Congress of the United States of America was irrelevant.

The president was in his glory talking about this "new kind of war" that lay ahead, a war for the very future of civilization. It would pit us against stateless terrorists who strike, blend in with the civilian population, then strike again. Despite all his talk of a new kind of war, the president would lead us into the old kind, the kind he and so many of the war hawks around him had dodged. He would put standing American armies in faraway cities, where enemies who look like civilians would pick us off one by one.

7

BEATING THE WAR DRUM

The political order in Washington was overthrown three times in the first three quarters of 2001, and dramatically so. President Clinton left office, taking his veto pen with him. That left Republicans in control of the White House and both houses of Congress. Then Senator Jim Jeffords bolted the party, putting Democrats back in control of the Senate, and disarming the tie-breaking vote that Vice President Cheney had wielded.

Finally, September 11 turned everything on its ear again. In the fear of the moment, Congress fully relinquished its duty to hold the executive branch to account. In effect, we had a one-branch system of government in America, and the man who headed it was taking us to war, even multiple wars.

On the day the Twin Towers came down in a heap and the Pentagon billowed black smoke, the commander in chief *was* the United States government. The chaotic vote on the resolution to authorize war in Afghanistan had demonstrated that both parties were prepared to yield all decision making to the president.

The news came on a sunny day in October. I was with a group of public officials walking in a Columbus Day parade in Westerly, Rhode Island, a largely Italian-American city that always turns out to honor that favorite son of Genoa, Cristoforo Colombo. Someone in the crowd shouted, "We've started bombing Afghanistan."

Like most Americans, I wanted to pursue the perpetrators behind the murderous acts of September 11. We were at a fork in the road, and I feared that a misguided response to September 11 would jeopardize the lasting peace that beckoned. A reporter for *The Providence Journal* called for a comment on the start of the war in Afghanistan. I was very aware that people had no patience for any questioning of the president, so I chose my words carefully.

"I'm behind the commander in chief but we have to be careful about inciting anti-American sentiment around the world," I said.

The region we were charging into was "a volatile mix of religion, nuclear weapons and oil production." The challenge would be to destroy our enemies while avoiding "a quagmire, a conflagration with no chance of success."

Bin Laden could be counted on to use our every miscalculation to recruit new adherents to his murderous ideology, I said.

"He is a diabolical character but he's not stupid. He's going to use this against us."

I never dreamed, then, that bin Laden would still be free six years later, but there was no doubt he was a crafty and formidable adversary. He had, after all, fought and defeated the Soviet war machine in Afghanistan.

Initially, our military effort in Afghanistan was an enormous success. We allied ourselves with the United Islamic Front for the Salvation of Afghanistan, the loose alliance of Tajiks, Hazaras, and Uzbeks in the north who were at war with the Taliban, and were armed by Iran and Russia. The White House and the media called the UIF the Northern Alliance, which was easier than explaining why we were joining Shia Islamic fundamentalists in a centuries-old fight against Sunni Islamic fundamentalists.

The Tajiks were primed to fight, given that just two days before September 11, Tunisian Arabs posing as television journalists had assassinated the Tajiks' most charismatic commander with a bomb concealed in a TV camera. Ahmad Shah Massoud, called the "Lion of Panjshir" for his exploits in battling the Soviet Army, was now the "Martyred Commander," and his men were eager to march on Kabul to avenge his death.

When they did so, under U.S. air cover, the Taliban melted into the mountains outside the capital, with our Tajik allies and American special operations troops in hot pursuit.

Here at home, my critics were in hot pursuit as well. The outpouring of venom on talk radio made it clear there was no room for a reasoned discussion in the critical weeks after September 11. Invited to appear on a radio show in Rhode Island, I advocated the dual-track response. To win, we needed to wage the present war and the future peace at the same time. I noted that the Founders meant to convey an important truth when they designed the Great Seal of the United States, which depicts a bald eagle with one claw grasping a quiver of arrows and the other grasping an olive branch. Both sets of "weapons" have their place.

Listeners went apoplectic at this. I do not think they held me responsible for the fact that the Founders had not loaded both of the eagle's claws with arrows; they just did not appreciate my bringing up the one with the olive branch. All incoming lines were jammed with irate, even hateful calls, and some talk-show hosts are only too happy to encourage such emotions, and ratings.

But everywhere I went, I continued to stress the need for a dual approach if we intended to succeed in ten, twenty, or thirty years. I said we had to be smart, not just quick on the trigger.

The host asked if I had heard rumblings that we might retaliate against Iraq because of September 11, and indeed I had. This was just ten days after the attacks. The White House was already bringing Iraq into the equation. The "clashists" who had come to power and were now setting American foreign policy were out to satisfy their ideology's strong appetite for war and conflict. They were quick to seize on September 11 as its latest rationale for regime change in Iraq. The extremists working on the Project for a New American Century had been itching to invade Iraq ever since President George H. W. Bush declared victory in Desert Storm without marching on Baghdad.

They started beating that drum right after the Gulf War ended. In the Defense Planning Guidance of 1992, presided over by then defense secretary Richard Cheney, the clashists outlined their vision for flexing American power in the post–cold war era. President George H. W. Bush quickly repudiated the imperial ideology expressed in the document, and back into the cocoon it went.

It had called for America to take preemptive, unilateral action against any nation on earth that might gain enough economic or military power to rival America as the undisputed world authority. When it was useful, we would declare ourselves the sole enforcer of U.N. resolutions; otherwise we would use international agreements on "an ad hoc basis" or disregard them altogether. It was an intellectually dishonest proposition. To the extremists, the only rule of law in the New American Century would be the rules that America made up to fit a given "problem" it wanted to resolve.

When the first President Bush left office, the radical right remained obsessed with Saddam. In a letter to President Clinton on January 26, 1998, the New American Century urged him to abandon our "containment" efforts and remove Saddam from power by force. Some of the adherents who signed the letter would later draw government paychecks under President George W. Bush: Elliott Abrams, Richard Armitage, John Bolton, Zalmay Khalilzad, Richard Perle, Donald Rumsfeld, and Paul Wolfowitz.

"The only acceptable strategy is one that eliminates the possibility that Iraq will be able to use or threaten to use weapons of mass destruction," they advised President Clinton in 1998. "If you act now to end the threat of weapons of mass destruction against the U.S. or its allies, you will be acting in the most fundamental national security interests of the country. If we accept a course of weakness and drift, we put our interests and our future at risk."

The choice was so simple, so clear, and, once they came to power and acted on these extremist views, so wrong.

On June 3, 1997, the New American Century published a "statement of principles" to guide the post–cold war era.

"Does the United States have the resolve to shape a new century favorable to American principles and interests?" they asked.

They advocated a massive defense buildup so we could "shape circumstances before crises emerge and meet new threats before they become dire."

America would read minds in the New American Century; it would foresee the future with superhuman clarity and act preemptively to preserve order.

"We need to accept responsibility for America's unique role in preserving and extending an international order friendly to our security, our prosperity and our principles."

I remember discussing these ideas with my confidants and we wondered: *Do they think our security, prosperity, and principles always coincide? Which one becomes paramount when they are in conflict? How does seeking conflict with hostile regimes necessarily extend an international order friendly to our security and our principles?*

As early as 1998, the New American Century was using the catchphrase "weapons of mass destruction" to take us down a very hazardous path. Of course, the real weapon of mass destruction is nuclear; but by whipping up fear over nonexistent chemical and biological weapons the Bush administration has actually harmed international efforts at nuclear *non*proliferation. With an extremist White House in power today, we have many unstable, hostile regimes sprinting to acquire nuclear weapons. In 1998 they claimed, absurdly, that President Clinton would be putting moderate Arab states at hazard if he failed to invade Iraq. Certainly, no one can deny now that our actions in Iraq have proven a far greater hazard to moderate Arab states than Saddam ever was after we annihilated his army in the Gulf War and effectively contained him.

In September 2000, the Project for a New American Century talked openly about needing some kind of cataclysm to occur before the public would accept its ideology. It said that "the process of transformation, even if it brings revolutionary change, is likely to be a long one, absent some catastrophic and catalyzing event—like a new Pearl Harbor."

A year later, on September 11, the clashists in the White House got just such a "new Pearl Harbor." We in Congress were ignorant of these intentions, despite the fact that these radical thinkers had openly publicized their aims. We had plenty of warning but did not identify and speak out against the threat they posed to international stability. I feel some guilt myself over this, that there was no debate on these questions as the Senate confirmed many of these people to appointive positions in the Bush administration. At the same time, where was the loyal opposition? We were not ready for this crowd, and we should have been.

In Afghanistan, our forces quickly routed the Taliban from Kabul, but then the war became a complex occupation and an exercise in nation building. With Osama bin Laden still at large, the White House shifted attention to Saddam, who clearly had nothing to do with September 11.

The work of the Senate did not stop while the president beat the war drum. In the spring of 2002 I went to China with a group of other senators and congressmen, and we met with trade officials and government leaders in Nanjing and Shanghai, then it was on to Beijing for an audience with Premier Zhu Rongji. My colleagues used a lecturing tone as we discussed such highly charged issues as relations with Taiwan, currency manipulation, and the Chinese black market in everything from movies to consumer products. When the seniority pecking order had worked its way down to me, I asked Premier Zhu: "What do you think about the growing chorus for war against Saddam Hussein?" The premier seemed taken aback. This was a different kind of question, unlike the gentle scoldings he had just heard. He almost waited for me to express my opinion first. I gave him no signal on what I thought. He looked at me a long time and said, simply, "As a friend . . . it is a mistake."

The brevity of his answer and the pause in the middle made it all the more powerful. He was that certain of its truth. It struck me as a heartfelt answer, candid and unequivocal.

"As a friend . . . it is a mistake."

We heard no such candor from witnesses that the administration sent to the Hill to testify in that first half of 2002. They had their scripted answers, and their orders: The commander in chief wanted to fight in Iraq.

Vice President Cheney assembled senators in small groups and brought them down to the Pentagon, of all places. It was an ever-brilliant piece of staging: a military setting, the vice president flanked by generals in crisp uniforms; the building still reverberating with reconstruction efforts after being hit by American Airlines Flight 77. There was no discussion encouraged. It was the same top-down style of meeting the vice president had with us when demanding that we support the tax cut. His mantra was: *The cost of inaction is higher than the cost of action.*

Our friends around the world knew the administration was tragically wrong on this. King Abdullah II of Jordan was alarmed enough to come to Washington and counsel the president against shifting attention from al-Qaeda and Afghanistan to regime change in Iraq. Abdullah has Iraq on his eastern border and the Arab-Israeli conflict on the west. Jordan was in the middle as Saddam lobbed Scud missiles at Israel during Desert Storm. I was content that he knew how to maintain a fragile stability in a volatile part of the world, and about the consequences of failure.

He warned of chaos, but President Bush thought he knew more about the region than the king of Jordan. The tragedy of September 11 was so fresh that it was easy for the clashists in the White House to sell Congress on opening a second front in Iraq. National Security Adviser Condoleezza Rice warned us about mushroom clouds appearing over American cities if we failed to march in lockstep behind the president. Secretary of State Colin Powell held up a sinister-looking vial of simulated anthrax at United Nations headquarters. President Bush and Vice President Cheney spoke falsely of yellowcake uranium from Africa making its way to secret nuclear weapons facilities in Iraq. The government was spreading fear, and fear of all kinds. In the Congress, the operative kind of fear, of course, is political fear. When Senator Jeffords quit the Republican Party and threw control of the Senate back to the Democrats, I thought he might have gained us a little time to do our jobs, to deliberate and slow down the president's rush to war. But the Democrats were not about to exercise that kind of leadership, so it did not matter that they controlled the Senate. Far from wanting to slow things down, they were throwing elbows in the rush to climb aboard the war train.

As the inevitable war vote approached, I asked for a meeting at CIA headquarters to speak with the professionals who were more likely than our high-ranking witnesses to tell me the truth, who would admit what they *did not* know about Iraq and Saddam. Getting inside the building would incidentally satisfy an old curiosity of mine. What really went on in the CIA citadel at Langley? When I was a teenager, I spent a few summers in nearby McLean when my father was secretary of the navy under President Richard Nixon. I often rode my horse, Tucker, a thoroughbred bay, around the well-guarded wire at Langley, wondering what our spies were up to in there. Now I had a reason to find out.

Expecting to be briefed by an intelligence analyst or two, I was led into a conference room where perhaps twenty sat waiting for me. I said, "Sooner or later, I have to vote on this war. Show me everything you have." What they had, I discovered as the meeting stretched into an hour, was next to nothing. And they knew it. It was apparent in their body language when they presented me with satellite photos, intelligence wire reports, and other classified materials. They showed me what they had with little comment and no enthusiasm. Someone handed me one of the infamous aluminum tubes, the kind that we were told Saddam was using to enrich weapons-grade uranium while plotting mushroom clouds over America, the "smoking gun" that Condoleezza Rice had warned about. I looked at the aluminum tube, looked at the analysts and thought, *I can go buy one of these at Adler's Hardware on Wick-enden Street in Providence.* A feeling of despair came over me. I was sick with visions of inevitability. Despite this absolute lack of proof, a reckless president and a spineless Congress were about to take us into an unnecessary and immoral war. Americans were going to die and be maimed for this. With the White House so eager to start that war, the intelligence experts at Langley had to either resign and write off their careers or play the administration's game. They played it that day, but I got the message.

Few members of Congress were willing to stand up to the schoolyard tough, and in the early morning hours of October 11, 2002, weeks before the critical midterm elections, he bullied them into declaring Saddam an imminent threat.

Today, we constantly hear yet another falsehood: *But everybody believed Saddam had weapons of mass destruction.* To the contrary, many spoke out about the unconvincing case the administration had made. The day the war started, I said to a reporter, "We won't find any weapons of mass destruction of a grossly threatening kind." We did our best to be heard, even if we did not prevail, and today many senators would like to forget that one quarter of their colleagues saw the president's hollow case for what it was. The late senator Paul Wellstone spoke out, even though he was in a tight reelection race. Carl Levin, chairman of the Armed Services Committee, crafted a commonsense way out via an amendment to the war resolution; the Levin Amendment was defeated and, within hours, the war authorization prevailed by virtually the same vote.

Senator Robert Byrd of West Virginia spoke with power and prescience on October 3, one week before Congress authorized the president to launch a second war. "Fie on this Congress," he shouted. He is an imperfect man, as are we all, but no one will ever say he was wrong on the war.

"Mr. President," he said, "Titus Livius, one of the greatest of Roman historians, said: 'All things will be clear and distinct to the man who does not hurry; haste is blind and improvident.' Blind and improvident. Blind and improvident. Congress would be wise to heed those words today, for as sure as the sun rises in the east, this country is embarking on a course of action with regard to Iraq that is both blind and improvident. We are rushing into war without fully discussing why, without thoroughly considering the consequences, or without making any attempt to explore what steps we might take to avert the conflict. The newly bellicose mood that permeates this White House is unfortunate, unfortunate all the more so because it is clearly motivated by campaign politics. Republicans are already running attack ads against Democrats on Iraq. Democrats favor fast approval of a resolution so they can change the subject to domestic economic problems.

"Why the rush? Is it our precious blood which will spew forth from our feeble veins? No. Those of you who have children, those of you who have grandchildren, those of you who have great-grandchildren should be thinking: It is the precious blood of the men and women who wear the uniform of these United States. That blood may flow in the streets of Iraq.

"What a shame," he thundered. "Fie upon the Congress. Fie upon some of the so-called leaders of the Congress for falling into this pit."

I spoke against the war, but no one said it better than Senator Byrd: Our "so-called leaders" were herding us into another Vietnam-style debacle. In the Republican caucus, blank faces stared back at me as I questioned the rush to war, and finally, in exasperation I said, "This is insanity!" But if the Democrats were buying into the war, how much more so my colleagues? They were ready to step off the cliff with the tough-talking president, trusting in his unbending confidence that he was right.

I believe that no war ever ends for a combat veteran; but, by 2002, Vietnam was finally over for most other Americans. We had healed and moved beyond the horrible images that defined the era: Vietnamese monks lighting themselves afire in the streets; a naked girl running down a road, her clothes burned away by napalm; bodies piled high in a ditch at My Lai; a suspected guerrilla executed by a pistol shot through the brain; students lying dead on the ground at Kent State University; the ignominious retreat of the last helicopter off the embassy roof.

Now come images of Abu Ghraib, the massacre at Haditha, and American body parts hanging from a bridge in Fallujah. In October of 2002, how could any Republican senator vote to send his country over the precipice again based on party loyalty? How could any Democratic senator follow suit out of political cowardice? When the president declared that Saddam was an imminent threat to America from seven thousand miles away, veteran lawmakers in both parties failed to fight back. They let the administration go unchallenged when it sent up witnesses who did their best to get us into the war the president wanted. I was infuriated when Secretary of State Colin Powell ran the clock as I questioned him in a hearing before the Senate Foreign Relations Committee on September 25, 2002, a month before the Iraq war vote. I had only seven minutes to draw out the fact that there was no evidence of an imminent threat or that Iraq would ever evolve into a threat.

I recalled for Secretary Powell that his predecessor, Secretary of State Madeleine Albright, had just told the committee that the war resolution was a mistake. "And all you have to do is run your hand over the black granite at the Vietnam Memorial to see what mistakes do," I said. I expected Powell, a Vietnam combat veteran, to lash out at me for that. Who was I to tell him about the awful cost of Vietnam? But the secretary kept his cool and stuck to the script. Ever the obedient soldier, he did the job he was sent up to the Hill to do. He gave windy answers, used my time, and said nothing that would cast doubt on the need for war in the newspaper headlines the next day.

On October 9, roughly thirty-six hours before the vote, I went to the Senate floor to say that the war authorization would serve those who believe in "ratcheting up the hatred."

In the end, even a majority of Senate Democrats voted for war. Only twenty-three senators voted to check a reckless president. I was the lone Republican among them.

8

CONGRESS STANDS DOWN

I find it surprising now, in 2008, how many Democrats are running for president after shirking their constitutional duty to check and balance this president. Being wrong about sending Americans to kill and be killed, maim and be maimed, is not like making a punctuation mistake in a highway bill. They argue that the president duped them into war, but getting duped does not exactly recommend their leadership. Helping a rogue president start an unnecessary war should be a career-ending lapse of judgment, in my view.

The top Democrats were at their weakest when trying to show how tough they were. They were afraid that Republicans would label them soft in the post–September 11 world, and when they acted on that political self-interest, they helped the president send thousands of Americans and uncounted innocent Iraqis to their doom.

Instead of talking tough, or meekly raising one's hand to support the tough talk, it is far more muscular, I think, to find out what is really happening in the world and have a debate about what we really need to accomplish. That is the hard work of governing, but it was swept aside once the fear, the war rhetoric, and the political conniving took over.

It was phenomenal how quickly key Democrats crumbled. They went down to meetings at the White House and the Pentagon and came back to the chamber ready to salute. With wrinkled brows they gravely intoned that *Saddam Hussein must be stopped.* Stopped from *what?* They had no conviction or evidence of their own. They were just parroting the administration's nonsense. They knew it could go terribly wrong; they also knew it could go terribly right. Which did they fear more? One Democratic senator, an opponent of the war, told me in confidence, "They're afraid the war will be over as fast as Gulf One. Few will die, the oil will flow, and gasoline will cost ninety cents a gallon."

Inexplicably, they had forgotten that in the Gulf War we had the international community with us, we were not out to occupy a large, hostile Muslim nation, and we were not already fighting a war in Afghanistan.

Many Democrats had opposed President George H. W. Bush's Gulf War. Now they were reluctant to oppose war again. They not only fell in line—they fought to get to the head of the line. They got it wrong on both Bush wars in Iraq.

On the Republican side, we had an extraordinary glimpse into the mentality of the man who was taking us to war. It happened one day in May 2002, just six months before the Iraq war vote, in the middle of the president's relentless campaign to turn public opinion in favor of a preemptive "defensive" strike against Saddam. The president met privately with Republican senators in the Mansfield Room in the Capitol.

Howard Fineman of *Newsweek* magazine had two sources in the caucus that day and reported the president's bizarre behavior and comments on May 27. Fineman described "a jut-jawed, disjointed discourse with a tinge of diatribe and a crescendo of podium pounding."

> The president dismissed questions about his administration's counterterrorism actions—or lack of them—before September 11 as mere Democratic partisanship. "I sniff some politics in the air," he scoffed. Then he wandered off to the Middle East, recounting a blunt Oval Office conversation with Ariel Sharon. He said he'd asked the Israeli leader if he really hated Yassir Arafat. Sharon had answered yes, according to the president. "I looked him straight in the eye and said, 'Well, are you going to kill him?' Sharon said no, to which the president said he'd replied, "That's good." Bush was just getting warmed up. "Now you guys really got me going," he said. He threatened to block the entire defense bill if it contained money for the controversial and costly Crusader artillery system. "I mean it. I'll veto it," he said tersely, glancing at Sen. Don Nickels of Oklahoma, where Crusader would be built. Bush ended with an attack on North Korean dictator Kim Jong Il. "He's starving his own people," Bush said, and imprisoning intellectuals in "a Gulag the size of Houston." The president called him a "pygmy" and compared him to "a spoiled child at a dinner table." Stunned senators didn't know quite what to make of the performance. "It was like in church, when the sermon goes on too long and you're not sure what the point is," one told Newsweek. "Nobody dared look at anybody else."

It was as if Mr. Fineman was in the room with us that day. I was astonished at the word-for-word accuracy of his report.

I was not the source, but now I knew that other Republican senators were alarmed, and, indeed, two were shaken enough to describe what they had witnessed to a prominent member of the national media. They wanted America to know.

For me, the president's remarks reinforced the conclusions I had already reached about him: that he was ruled by emotion and had a juvenile streak in his personality. His tirade against the North Korean dictator was positively unhinged. Kim Jong Il is a dangerous man; he needs to be restrained by serious men and women who are skilled in the art of statecraft. I could not imagine what national interest the president thought he was serving by calling this adversary a "pygmy" and "a spoiled child at the dinner table."

When the president shifted gears suddenly and recounted the conversation with Ariel Sharon, the talk of killing Yassir Arafat, he spoke in an exaggerated Texas twang I had never heard him use before. The story was a non sequitur; I had no idea what the president meant to communicate to Republicans by telling it.

A year earlier, when I had met the president one-on-one in the Oval Office, I came away associating this word with him: unpresidential. Now he had behaved that way in front of the entire Republican caucus. And someone in the room had been alarmed enough to describe it virtually word for word to a reporter. I thought, maybe *this* will slow the rush to war. I thought there would be introspection in the caucus, at last, as we confronted this momentous war vote. *Might this be the event that finally gets the Senate leading again?* It cried out for us to check and balance the White House and examine the commander in chief's purported evidence of an Iraqi threat and, indeed, his fitness to serve.

When I saw the Fineman article I knew the White House would be furious. There was no staff in the Mansfield Room that day. The president must have felt he could speak freely because a Republican senator would never embarrass him by talking out of school. Now it was clear to all that at least two Republican senators had done exactly that.

This was a fork in the road, in May 2002. At this historic time, we in the Senate had a choice between shepherding Berlusconi's "age of lasting peace" or yielding to the clashists' vision of perpetual conflict. The impending Iraq war vote would take us down the latter road. The president's leadership was never questioned within the party, but now fifty of us had witnessed a disturbingly stark reason to question him.

In the days that followed, Republicans focused their energy on identifying the leakers who had talked to *Newsweek*. I knew that anger would manifest itself, but I hoped it would be short-lived and we could soon get down to talking seriously among ourselves about stopping the rush to war and taking power back from this president.

It was not to be. The party was too immersed in the diversion, the effort to name the GOP senators who had embarrassed the president.

In 2002, we were doing more than mulling the Iraq war authorization and reeling from a presidential diatribe. We were busy combining twenty-two federal agencies into the militaristically named Department of Homeland Security, or, as Senator Dick Durbin of Illinois once called it, chuckling, "The Department of the Fatherland Security."

Democrats were worried that President Bush, while enlarging the federal bureaucracy, would deny some Homeland Security employees the collective bargaining rights of other federal employees. This sparked a real battle in the fall of 2002. The Democrats controlled the Senate, and with my vote they held up the Homeland Security bill over the union issue. Democratic Senator John Breaux of Louisiana was a key negotiator in the effort to find common ground and get the bill moving again. I arrived early for a meeting in his office, and while we waited for other negotiators to arrive, I asked senator Breaux whether he realized that holding up Homeland Security over union rights was going to hurt some of his most vulnerable Democrats, among them, Max Cleland in Georgia and Jean Carnahan in Missouri. Breaux dismissed it, and was confident the Democrats would retain the majority. But the election did revolve on security, and, in the end, senators Cleland and Carnahan were unseated. Republicans spent millions on campaign ads that flayed Cleland and Carnahan as unpatriotic, caring more about collective bargaining rights than whether terrorists kill Americans. Again, the Democrats miscalculated; the ads turned both races and cost the Democrats the majority. Senator Cleland had lost his legs and right arm while serving in Vietnam. It was absurd to question his patriotism, but the Republican National Committee ads made the charge stick. The Republican victor, Saxby Chambliss, is a good man and would go out of his way to help in my 2006 re-election bid, but I missed the good-natured Max Cleland in the chamber. He had been a daily reminder of real sacrifice and love of country.

Democrat Tom Daschle was a skillful minority leader in 2000. He helped win the seats that resulted in a fifty-fifty Senate, and then went on to become majority leader by wooing Jim Jeffords of Vermont to quit the Republican Party. But the Daschle genius for strategy evaporated as the Twin Towers came crashing down. He put his two most vulnerable senators in a fatal predicament by demanding that they support the unions and hold up the Homeland Security bill. In the campaigns in Georgia and Missouri it did not count that senators Cleland and Carnahan had voted to authorize the war in Iraq; their Republican opponents labeled them soft on terrorism because of their stance on the union issue alone. The Democrats lost control of the Senate by reverting to form and catering to their labor constituency in a time of national emergency. They had a knack for standing up on the wrong issues and standing down on the right ones. I would rather have seen the loyal opposition and Max Cleland leading the charge against another Vietnam instead of the cause of labor rights in Homeland Security.

Besides senators Cleland and Carnahan, we also lost Democrat Paul Wellstone of Minnesota that year. He was in a fierce battle for reelection with the energetic and bright former mayor of St. Paul, Republican Norm Coleman. Tragically, Wellstone along with members of his family and staff died in a plane crash days before the 2002 election. At the last minute, Democrats fielded former vice president Walter Mondale in his place.

The surviving members of the Wellstone family held a memorial service for Paul in the Williams Arena at the University of Minnesota. I and many of my Senate colleagues were among the twenty thousand mourners. The Wellstone family was overcome with grief and not thinking clearly that day. When one of them spoke of healing the partisan divide in Washington, the memorial service took a political turn that generated a backlash and severely hurt Democratic efforts to keep the Wellstone seat in the Senate. Trent Lott was in the arena with us that day. When the Wellstone family mentioned his name, the TV cameras sought him out in the audience, where he sat with his wife, Trisha. Suddenly their faces filled the giant screen. It was an embarrassing moment for all, and unfair to Trent. There were precious few things that he and Paul had agreed upon; but Trent had made the trip to Minnesota to pay his respects to a fellow battler, not to be held up as a symbol of all that ails the Senate. That awkward turn in the memorial service did a lot to hurt the Mondale candidacy and helped to elect Norm Coleman.

In South Dakota that year, Democratic senator Tim Johnson won reelection over GOP challenger John Thune by 0.15 percent of the vote. All night long, it seemed that Thune had unseated Johnson in an upset; but the race turned when the late vote came in from the western counties, where Native Americans voted for Democrats overwhelmingly. But even with Thune's narrow loss, the Senate was back in Republican hands by two votes.

The pendulum kept marking the beat of our lives in that charged political chamber. We had gone from the Clinton veto to a Bush monopoly on power to a Democratic Senate courtesy of Jim Jeffords and now back to Republican control after the first election cycle of the post–September 11 era.

We were all tested as we watched the control of power in Washington shift on one improbable event after another, with the fate of the nation hanging in the balance.

9

THE PARTY OF OLD KING COAL

Worldwide, many think one of the gravest threats we face on earth is climate change. The president had promised to lead on that when he pledged to regulate carbon dioxide emissions. After taking office, he reversed course. It became a special point of pride in the administration that it would do nothing to address greenhouse gasses.

I've never heard the president explain why. He had made his pledge in a major campaign speech on September 29, 2000. His words on "A Comprehensive National Energy Policy" raised false hopes among voters who care about clean air. He said he would recognize carbon dioxide as a pollutant emitted by coal-fired power plants.

"With the help of Congress, environmental groups and industry, we will require all power plants to meet clean air standards in order to reduce emissions of sulfur dioxide, nitrogen oxide, mercury and carbon dioxide within a reasonable period of time."

His message was unequivocal, and for a Republican it was a bold one. Environmentalists had long advocated that the federal government regulate the enormous amounts of carbon dioxide emitted by electricity-generating power plants, because of the strong science that links carbon dioxide emissions to climate change.

Once in office, the president named Christie Todd Whitman, former Republican governor of New Jersey, to head the Environmental Protection Agency. In her new role as administrator, Whitman made many public pronouncements on the coming effort to regulate carbon dioxide emissions. It seemed Republicans, often accused of being in league with polluters, might finally challenge the popular notion that only Democrats care about the air we breathe. After all, it was President Richard Nixon who had signed into law the nation's first clean air legislation.

The United States has often been called the Saudi Arabia of coal. That fossil fuel is a vast and important resource if we can mine it and burn it without harming the environment. Even some members of the coal industry agree that it is only a matter of time before we regulate carbon dioxide and that America should take the lead in developing clean coal technologies. Many Republican leaders accept the science—they just do not plan to act on it. However, a fringe segment of the GOP actively denies the science.

Senate Republicans took great delight when President Bush, early in his administration, recanted on regulating carbon dioxide. I was a witness to EPA administrator Whitman's humiliation on this point.

On February 26, Ms. Whitman said on *Crossfire*, to conservative commentator Robert Novak: "George Bush was very clear during the course of the campaign that he believed in a multi-pollutant strategy, and that includes CO_2, and I have spoken to that. He also has been very clear that the science is good on global warming. It does exist. There is a real problem that we as a world face from global warming and to the extent that introducing CO_2 to the discussion is going to have an impact on global warming, that's an important step to take."

Then, in the interview with Mr. Novak, she continued to emphasize the clarity of the president's campaign pledge, oblivious to the thin ice under her feet.

"He talked about that during the campaign. He brought up the multi-pollutant strategy during the campaign and a lot of energy groups will tell you, and the energy companies, the utilities will tell you that they can [control CO_2 emissions]. It's going to be difficult. There will be challenges there but there are ways that we can get to a multi-pollutant strategy on energy that would allow for energy and still meet some of these demands and the needs that we need to meet on global warming."

Just two weeks later, on March 13, Vice President Cheney told the Republican caucus at our regular weekly lunch that the administration had decided to reverse course on the carbon dioxide pledge. Contrary to the president's campaign pledge, there would be no such regulation of coal-burning utilities on his watch. A tremendous cheer went up from the caucus assembled in the Mansfield Room, with shouts of *Hoo-hah!* and *Hoo-rah!* As the cheers rang out, a senator, I am not certain who, shouted, "Somebody better tell Christie!"

Governor Whitman was told, and continued to serve.

President Bush, true to the Cheney proclamation, soon offered a clean air bill that made a mockery of its own title: "Clear Skies." Senator Jim Jeffords sponsored the Democrats' competing legislation after he left the Republican Party and was named chairman of the Environment and Public Works Committee.

Because the Jeffords bill had no chance of attracting enough Republican votes to gain passage, Senator Tom Carper, Democrat of Delaware, and I tried to bridge the gap between the Bush and Jeffords bills with a middle-ground proposal. We drew some support from the Republican side, from Lamar Alexander of Tennessee, Judd Gregg of New Hampshire, and others, but President Bush was uninterested in compromise. In the end, all three bills went nowhere.

While defeating efforts to control greenhouse gasses and ceding that important issue to the Democrats, the Republican caucus was obsessed with opening up the Arctic National Wildlife Refuge to oil exploration. We had vote after vote on drilling in ANWR, and many of them close.

It was a top priority for the clashists; they had to show the environmentalists who was boss by opening up this unique wilderness to oil exploration.

In committee, we heard conflicting descriptions of the refuge. Environmentalists described it as lush and teeming with wildlife; the oil interests said it was a wasteland, one that, in any event, they would leave in the same state in which they found it.

Several members of congress decided to see ANWR for ourselves during the monthlong congressional recess of August 2002. The Wilderness Society had offered to guide us on a three-day trek north of the Brooks Range, and then fly us into Prudhoe Bay, where we could meet with industry executives to hear their side of the story.

We met up in Arctic Village, a native settlement in central Alaska. There were members of the Wilderness Society there, congressmen Rush Holt and Sherrod Brown, some members of their staffs, and my wife, Stephanie, and I.

Two De Havilland single-engine planes ferried us north, over the inhospitable Brooks Range. Once we cleared the summits, I was stunned at the vista that lay before us. There were fifteen miles of rolling grasslands below, stretching from the north face of the mountains, over the foothills, and down to the Beaufort Sea. It was a true Arctic prairie at the top of America, three hundred miles north of the Arctic Circle.

I never expected that.

As our pilot banked, looking for a place to land, we spooked a cinnamon-colored grizzly bear. He bounded away through the brush as the plane touched down. We unloaded tents and camping supplies and spent the next three days seeing the wonders of ANWR. The witnesses who had described it as a wasteland had no idea what they were talking about.

We saw grizzly bears every day, and, fortunately, never had an encounter with them. Everywhere we saw ptarmigan, a kind of Arctic prairie chicken, and the place was alive with ground squirrels. The herds of caribou and musk oxen had already come through, as evidenced by the ubiquitous droppings they left behind. It struck me that people who called ANWR "the American Serengeti" had gotten it exactly right.

Airborne again, we flew west toward Prudhoe Bay to see the impressive drilling operations built there in the 1970s and meet with industry advocates. The geography quickly changed from prairie grasslands to marshy tundra. Here, the roads had to be built up over the elevation of the northern marshlands.

Advocates of drilling in ANWR gave us a presentation and said they could go into the refuge in winter, when the ground was frozen solid, thereby eliminating the need for a similar network of roads. They could work on frozen ground, do their drilling, then leave without a trace.

I kept an open mind and listened carefully. I know we need oil to run our economy. At the same time, the unexpected beauty of the refuge was hard to forget. I had lived in Canada on the racetrack circuit for seven years and also wanted to take the Canadian view into account. The caribou herds that pass through ANWR migrate in and out of Canada as well. The Canadian government opposes any oil development in ANWR that might disrupt the migration patterns of this international phenomenon. I did not see any harm in promoting good relations with our neighbor by recognizing the herd as more than just an American issue.

We spent a few days in Prudhoe Bay, meeting people who had braved the trip there overland, on the Alaska Highway. It was literally the end of the road, and I had to admire people who had gotten there in beat-up cars and trucks, peering out of windshields turned into spiderwebs by flying gravel. They had made it.

Some of these northern travelers dove into the frigid Beaufort Sea, just to say they had. Each one collected a certificate from the locals to document their hardiness for the folks back home.

Our hotel in Prudhoe Bay was really a collection of mobile homes that had been trucked in and linked together. Our "concierge," as we called him, a bearded man who sat behind the desk in the mud-caked "lobby," warned us about going out at night.

It was as light at three in the morning as at three in the afternoon, and he thought we might be tempted to see the sights if we could not sleep.

"Watch out for Toby," he said.

"Toby" was a grizzly that had moved in off the tundra and taken to foraging in town.

About three months later, I saw a short filler article in *The New York Times* about a nuisance bear in Prudhoe Bay. He had been darted and relocated several times, but he kept coming back to what he thought should be bear country.

The article said the bear, dubbed Toby by the locals, had finally been shot, in the interest of public safety.

Conflicts like that are inevitable whenever we go into wilderness areas to bring out the resources we need. If we open up ANWR to drilling, there are bound to be conflicts between the crews bringing out the oil and bears that want to get in among the mobile homes and find some chow. When I put down the article, I thought, *Let's leave just one place off limits.* A Republican president, Dwight Eisenhower, had signed ANWR into existence; I was not about to be a part of undoing his vision.

If ANWR is a wildlife refuge, wildlife should find sanctuary there, by definition. Letting in the oil companies while still calling it a refuge struck me as dishonest. It is also wrong that the same lawmakers who are so eager to drill in ANWR consistently thwart efforts to curb our oil consumption. I always supported the role of the federal government in reducing oil consumption, and the most effective mechanism is to raise the gas mileage standards that car manufacturers must meet. The Corporate Average Fuel Economy (CAFE) rules were enacted in 1975, after the shock of the Arab oil embargo of two years earlier. In my tenure in Washington, there were frequent votes on raising the mileage standards as well as closing the loophole that exempts sport utility vehicles from the CAFE standards. The loophole was designed to help the American Motors Corporation, which was teetering on the edge of bankruptcy at the time. One of AMC's bestsellers was the Jeep Wagoneer, which Congress wanted to keep profitable, given that the federal government was guaranteeing loans to the ailing company. The loophole has since accommodated SUVs that dwarf the Wagoneer, the mammoth Esplanades, Expeditions, Hummers, and the like. On vote after vote, we failed to close the SUV loophole and raise mileage standards overall. Unfortunately, American carmakers fight these efforts to mandate fuel-efficient vehicles and, predictably, foreigners are beating us in the marketplace just as they did in the 1970s. The industry has a history of fighting innovation. It fought mandatory seat belts and the phase-out of leaded gasoline just as adamantly as an increase in CAFE standards. The carmakers pressured their senators, particularly in Michigan, to abandon their usual wise stance on environmental matters and resist fuel economy.

After we returned from ANWR on the Alaskan North Slope, it was not long before the leadership called yet another vote to allow drilling there. Republican senators Ted Stevens and Frank Murkowski, both of Alaska, strongly advocated a yea vote.

Before that vote I went to the Senate floor with photos of our trip, enlarged to poster size. Again, members in favor of drilling described ANWR as a wasteland, but I gave an impassioned speech to the contrary, complete with photos. Senator Stevens was irate that I would dare to challenge him on this. He let his anger get the best of him and gave a somewhat threatening response to my floor speech. I shrugged it off and headed for the Senate subway to return to my office. A veteran reporter trailed me down through those narrow corridors, his eyes wide at the vociferous rebuke that Senator Stevens had given me. He said, "This goes back to the eighties when your dad voted against Stevens for majority leader, in favor of Bob Dole." I got a chuckle out of that, a reporter as the Greek chorus, whispering a side commentary as the ANWR drama entered Act III. My father and Senator Stevens had gone to Harvard Law School together, Class of 1950. I assumed that Senator Stevens would soon get over my heresy, and he did; but, the relentless quest to drill in ANWR had taken on a symbolic dimension far beyond the actual value of the oil. These were some of the most pitched environmental battles that occurred in my time in the Senate. The native tribe in the region, the Gwich'in, would faithfully make the long trek to Washington before every vote, and they would plead with us to leave intact the refuge and their way of life. We often prevailed by razor-thin margins, and, to my party's credit, senators John McCain, Mike DeWine, Gordon Smith, Susan Collins, and Norm Coleman were key players in protecting the Arctic National Wildlife Refuge.

10

MISSION ACCOMPLISHED

In 2003, the Jim Jeffords defection had come and gone and the Bush administration had both houses of Congress back under Republican control. This was the start of the presidential cycle, and even for a nakedly political administration the partisan calculating became exponentially greater. On April 3, American forces were in Baghdad. Iraqis cheered as our soldiers pulled down one of the biggest statues Saddam had erected to glorify himself as the dictator of Mesopotamia. A month later, on May 1, President Bush made his triumphant landing on the aircraft carrier *Abraham Lincoln,* under the "Mission Accomplished" banner, and senators were eager to see the new Iraq firsthand. At the invitation of Senator Mitch McConnell of Kentucky, I visited Afghanistan and Iraq in October of 2003. Other Republicans on the factfinding tour were Conrad Burns of Montana, the late Craig Thomas of Wyoming, and Larry Craig of Idaho.

On our way into Afghanistan, we landed in Islamabad,

Pakistan, a country where Islam is the official state religion. There were people everywhere. Every street and marketplace and bus stop was teeming with people buying and selling, and not just the goods of everyday life; they were buying and selling ideas that will determine whether America wins or loses the fight against Islamic extremism. The shooting fronts were in Afghanistan and Iraq, but I knew the war could just as well hinge on what happened in Pakistan, a young and volatile country carved out of what used to be known as British India.

Pakistan is the sixth most populous country in the world, with as many people as the behemoth Russia to its north. There are more than 160 million Pakistanis, one for every two Americans in a country the size of Texas, and most are young and still forming their ideas about the world. They have nuclear weapons and the rocket technology to deliver them into the bordering nations of Iran, Afghanistan, China, and India.

Every action we take in this Muslim nation tends to push Pakistanis to one side or the other of our roster of friends and enemies. In my time in Washington, I saw the Bush administration doing things that were virtually certain to promote extremism in this strategic country between the Middle East and the subcontinent. In 2007, Vice President Cheney went to Pakistan to pressure General Pervez Musharraf into increasing Pakistani military efforts in the lawless tribal areas on the Afghan border. Cheney hardly needed to mention to the general the $10 billion that the United States had doled out to him since September 11, most of it in military aid.

Anyone who attempts to rule such a country as Pakistan wants to suppress radical elements without drawing them into a mutual suicide pact. Common sense tells you that deals are made. *You leave me alone, I leave you alone.*

At a hearing in the Foreign Relations Committee, as a State Department official testified in sonorous tones on the hunt for bin Laden, I nudged Senator Chuck Hagel and said, "Have they checked the apartment next to Musharraf's?"

When Vice President Cheney went to Pakistan to browbeat the general to get tougher on Afghan fighters taking sanctuary in his country, I knew it would not be long before a "top Taliban commander" was captured in Pakistan, then everything would settle back down to the status quo.

We saw this routine for years with organized crime in New England. When the pressure was on, the Mafia would serve up an expendable stooge who was making trouble for the mob anyway, then it would be business as usual.

As chairman of the Foreign Relations Subcommittee on the Middle East and South Asia, I met with various delegations of Pakistani officials, including some political opponents of Musharraf's. On one occasion, I floated the same cynical scenario I had joked about with Senator Hagel: Was the man who had slaughtered nearly three thousand people on September 11 really hiding in a cave on the mountainous border between Afghanistan and Pakistan, or was he sipping tea out of a silver cup in the apartment next to Musharraf's?

The political passions of my visitors were unleashed, with great animation. *Of course there's a deal! We all know that's true!*

I had baited them with hyperbole, but my point was that the truth can be more complex than meets the eye.

I was aware of attempts on Musharraf's life. With a wink

to my foreign relations staffer, Mark Silverman, I mentioned one attempt in particular and said, "That had to be staged. Musharraf wanted to send a message to Washington." My guests poured out detailed descriptions of how the roads converged at the "attack site," how no one who wanted to kill Musharraf would pick that spot; it would never work.

Set aside the fact that people died in the attempts on Musharraf's life; I was interested in seeing the world through my visitors' eyes for a moment. Here was a window into what they were really thinking behind the veneer of diplomatic language they normally used.

I thought back to that meeting when, in 2006, the Bush administration was proposing to help India build nuclear generators to power its economy and improve living standards for its one billion citizens. President Bush had some of us over to the West Wing to build support for the U.S.-India nuclear energy deal. It was clear to me what we were trying to accomplish: We did not want India relying on oil. We especially did not want it relying on Iranian oil. Essential trade of that sort could lead to troublesome political alliances between India and Iran, with the powder keg that is Pakistan sandwiched in between.

When I had an opportunity to speak to the president, I stressed that any deal with India must not jeopardize stability in Pakistan. The president nodded gravely and said he was fully aware that General Musharraf had nearly been assassinated.

At dawn on that October day in 2003, our Senate delegation flew out of Islamabad in a C-130 cargo plane and headed northwest over the Hindu Kush, into Afghanistan. I had never seen anything like the geography below. The land seemed alive and contorted, as if you could see from the air how Afghanistan was pressured from all sides in this crossroads of civilizations, bordered by China, Iran, Pakistan, and the former Soviet Republics to the north, Turkmenistan, Uzbekistan, and Tajikistan. It seemed caught between the continents of Europe, Asia, and Africa. The geography mirrored the political realities.

We landed at Bagram Air Base just outside the Afghan capital. After briefings in Kabul we headed south to Kandahar. Everywhere we went, we saw a truly international presence in this former Soviet battleground. The many nations of NATO were well represented in the effort to build a post-Soviet, post-Taliban society.

I was struck by the Afghans' simple way of living, which seemed out of another millennium. Mud and clay buildings blended into a brown landscape. You could turn in one direction or another and see little if any evidence of the modern world. But in every Afghan face we saw an unmistakable pride in their place in history.

From there it was on to Kuwait for a flight to Baghdad. Once on the ground in this hotter of our two shooting wars in the region, we donned flak jackets and joined a convoy of a half-dozen armored vehicles setting out on the ten-mile ride into the fortified Green Zone. The insurgency was clearly active, though not what it would become three and four years later. In the improvised explosive device the insurgency had found its devastating weapon of choice. The odds were, an American who went home dead or wounded had been attacked with an IED. Our convoy traveled with army

Humvees fore and aft, both with a heavy machine gun swiveling about, scanning for any threat.

The military briefed us in the Green Zone, then our escorts took us to see a school that U.S. forces were refurbishing. Along the way, our convoy passed a soccer field where some Iraqi lads were kicking a ball. The field was mostly gravel, very unlike the green, well-watered fields of America. We wound through the narrow streets and passed a field that looked much like the first one, where boys like the others kicked a ball in clouds of dust. After more winding streets, another field, another game, and I realized we were passing the same field for the third time. We were lost and going in circles. Our drivers stopped to ask directions from the local people and some Iraqi women came out of their houses. I do not speak Arabic, but it seemed to me they gave heartfelt greetings to the Americans. Eventually, we found the school and had our tour, and then it was on to a local power plant. The same Iraqis who had been running it under Saddam were back at work coaxing kilowatts from reluctant machinery. The plant, and every other piece of infrastructure we saw, had not had any maintenance in a decade, the result, our escorts said, of the U.N. sanctions imposed after the Gulf War.

After Baghdad, we flew to Mosul in northern Iraq and met with General David Petraeus. He was respected in Mosul, so much so that he was later named commander of all U.S. forces in Iraq, when the situation was most dire.

In that fall of 2003, we were able to fly in helicopters and move freely on the ground with minimal security. Yes, we wore flak jackets, but I had expected Iraq to seem much more dangerous and chaotic. After all, five hundred Americans had lost their lives here, and insurgents armed with a truck bomb had killed United Nations special representative Sérgio Vieira de Mello in an attack on U.N. headquarters in August. I was surprised at how calm things seemed. As we traveled back on the main artery between the airport and the Green Zone, my head snapped around as a bus full of Iraqi children went by us in the opposite direction. All hands waved from the open windows, flashing the thumbs-up sign at the American convoy. This image went into the mix of conflicting information. The America I know and love would never launch an unjustified war in an alien land and culture, but maybe some good would come out of it after all. I saw a glimmer of hope for Iraq in those smiling, waving children, but was concerned about the war we had left behind. Afghanistan was the forgotten front, and that was the predominant impression I took from the trip to the region. We were fully committed in Iraq but had turned our back on Afghanistan and left it largely to the Germans, British, and other NATO forces to carry the effort forward.

A year later, the war in Iraq was unraveling, American casualties were on the increase, the 2004 presidential election was in full swing, and no one in Washington was talking about whether we were winning or losing the fight for Afghanistan.

I wanted to see someone oppose President Bush in the Republican primary. The alternative was to watch him spend the entire primary season in his comfort zone, speaking in slogans to friendly, handpicked Republican audiences. I thought we might finally have the debate that Congress had avoided in 2002. I considered doing it myself. In the fall of 2003, part of me thought it was cowardly to oppose the president on so many issues and then not oppose him head-on as he sought renomination. But reality trumped reason. On a Sunday morning in December 2003, I walked into the Blueberry Hill Store in Exeter, Rhode Island, to buy a newspaper. The owner, Clark Whitford, trusts his customers to make their own change from a till on the counter, by a wall decorated with photos of tractors and cows. There are always people there, staking out the chairs inside the store and the roadside porch. That day, the Sunday morning regulars were drinking coffee while glued to the TV screen. Our forces had dragged a bearded Saddam out of a dusty hole in the ground near Tikrit, the Sunni stronghold of his birth. The once-mighty dictator was photographed as a doctor examined his eyes, mouth, and ears. The strongman who had fancied himself a regional leader of pan-Arab nationalism was reduced to an utterly humiliated figure.

President Bush was triumphant for a few weeks following Saddam's capture. Anyone who had jumped into the New Hampshire primary against him would have been up against this moment of glory. As always, timing is everything in politics. For people inclined to support the president, he once again stood ten feet tall, the leadoff conqueror in chief of the new American century.

On the Democratic side, Governor Howard Dean of Vermont had caught fire. He hammered the president on his conduct of the war and came from nowhere to become the frontrunner. Many of his rivals for the Democratic nomination had voted to authorize the president to launch the war in Iraq, which hurt their credibility with Americans who wanted us out of the deepening chaos. However, the Democratic establishment grew wary of Dean, doubting that the firebrand had national appeal. It went instead with John Kerry, who had combat experience in Vietnam and showed he could win votes in Iowa.

In the months ahead, events seemed to turn in Kerry's favor. He racked up wins in one primary after another. No one was cheering the capture of Saddam anymore. Instead, that spring, they were repulsed by photos of dead American contractors, their charred remains hanging from a bridge over the Euphrates River in Fallujah, in the Sunni Triangle. Weeks later we were confronted with photos of Iraqis undergoing grotesque forms of torture and sexual abuse at the hands of the 372nd Military Police Company guarding Abu Ghraib prison, twenty miles west of Baghdad.

These sickening spectacles were broadcast around the world. When I saw smiling Iraqis dancing and cheering on the bridge, I was left wondering, *Who are the real Iraqis? Were they on the bus that passed our convoy in Baghdad, or are they cheering the savagery on that bridge over the Euphrates?*

American soldiers had asked a similar question in Saigon forty years earlier. There was no one "real Iraqi," just as there had been no one real Vietnamese. They were friend and foe at the same time.

Even against the backdrop of Abu Ghraib and Fallujah, the Kerry campaign never captured the antiwar fervor that Governor Dean had so successfully energized.

John Kerry flopped on his first important decision as the Democratic nominee. Choosing Senator John Edwards as a running mate did nothing to diversify the Democratic ticket. In the end, Edwards could not even deliver North Carolina, his home state. The Bush team knew they had enormous political difficulties ahead in the fall, as the occupation of Iraq continued to deteriorate. They went with their trusted blueprint for victory: Energize the base and drive up the turnout from that segment of America only. The president had pledged in 2000 to heal wounds and bring America together again—to be a uniter, not a divider. But, in 2004, he set out to generate the anger and fear needed to gain even a razor-thin plurality and win a second term. During the campaign, the Senate did not debate how we were losing the peace in Iraq; we debated putting new restrictions on abortion, drilling for oil in the Arctic National Wildlife Refuge, and cutting taxes again, despite the record deficits caused by the 2001 cuts and two foreign wars. The Bush-Cheney ticket and the Republican political leadership wanted us taking these wedge issues into the 2004 campaign. The president was skilled in the art of dividing America and motivating his base. Senator Kerry, meanwhile, seemed bent on demoralizing his own. As late as August of 2004, he famously declared he would vote again to authorize the Iraq War, despite that the premise for the war had been proven false, and despite the daily, needless carnage.

He seemed to be doing his best to let the air out of his own campaign.

Given what the Bush-Cheney machine had done to Senator John McCain in South Carolina four years earlier, Senator Kerry should have known it would be a brass-knuckles fight in 2004. When the so-called Swift Boat Veterans for Truth attacked his service in Vietnam, Kerry's response was flat-footed and tepid. Then he allowed himself to be photographed windsurfing in Nantucket "in Spandex," as Senator Zell Miller sneered. He was incessantly ridiculed and savaged.

I was no Kerry supporter, certainly, but it was incomprehensible to me that a man of his intelligence could not seem to get traction against a president who joked about the vain search for weapons of mass destruction in Iraq, a search that had gotten so many Americans killed and wounded.

On March 24, 2004, the Radio and Television Correspondents Association had its annual black-tie dinner at the Hilton in Washington. I was there that night when President Bush did a skit about searching for weapons of mass destruction. Photos of him looking under and behind the furniture in the West Wing flashed on a screen as he said, "Those weapons of mass destruction have got to be somewhere. . . . Nope, no weapons over there. . . . Maybe under here." The correspondents laughed and guffawed.

The president had started a war on the false premise that Saddam had weapons of mass destruction and was about to unleash them on America. Now he appeared to be making fun of himself and his war, but he was actually making fun of anyone who used the WMD issue against him. In joking about weapons that never existed, I realized, he was making a joke of anyone who kept harping on the false premise for the war. George Bush never makes fun of criticisms that are off point; he mocks the ones that hit home. That tends to disarm them. But when a president jokes about the biggest mistake of perhaps any presidency in American history, this is a quantum leap beyond the tasteless and tone-deaf humor one often hears in Washington. Here the president used his reason for starting a costly and interminable war as a punch line. Whenever he looked behind a chair or under a couch and announced, "Nope, no weapons here!" the message I heard was: *Suckers. You believed me. The joke is on you.*

Four years earlier, Richard Cheney had lionized Governor Bush to the Republican convention in Philadelphia: "A man of principle, a man of honor. On the first hour of the first day he will restore decency and integrity to the Oval Office."

I had voted for George W. Bush, but resolved not to make that mistake again in 2004. It was a problem because I had always voted the straight Republican ticket and wanted to be able to say I had never voted Democratic when a Republican was on the ballot. When I was young, I watched my father recruit Republicans to run for office in Rhode Island, from local races to statewide general officers. Often we knew our candidates were sacrificial lambs who would be crushed by a powerful Democratic incumbent, but I loyally supported the candidate, who frequently would come away, we all knew, with 21 percent of the vote and the bruises to show for it.

I knew I could not vote for John Kerry in 2004. His campaign had cast real doubt on his judgment as far as I was concerned.

I planned to write in a Republican candidate of my choosing.

That October, I gave a speech before an environmental group in the auditorium at *The Providence Journal* building, in downtown Providence. Major media were there because I had been speaking out about the vice president's energy policy bill, his insistence on drilling for oil in the Arctic National Wildlife Refuge, on denying climate change, and on resisting calls for higher mileage standards for new cars.

Naturally, someone in the audience got around to asking the logical question. *How can you vote for George Bush when you oppose everything he wants to do or isn't doing about the environment?*

Reporters scribbled the question in their notebooks and looked up for my answer. I said, "Who said I'm voting for George Bush?"

The feeding frenzy was on.

No one asked me whose name I would write on my ballot, and I had not decided on a name in any event. The next day, my press secretary, Stephen Hourahan, suggested that I vote for the president's father, George H. W. Bush. Before the words were even out, I knew I would do just that. Voting for the president's father would make the point that there was nothing personal in my criticism of the president. I just could not abide his habit of saying one thing and doing another.

On election day, I wrote the name George H. W. Bush on my ballot. Then I underlined the "H."

In the wee hours after the polls closed, when Ohio declared its electoral votes for the president, the 2002 strategy of fear and division had triumphed again for Republicans in 2004. Most notably, the party swept all five open seats in the Deep South; seats vacated by Democrats John Edwards in North Carolina, Fritz Hollings in South Carolina, Zell Miller in Georgia, Bob Graham in Florida, and John Breaux in Louisiana. This completed the historic shift in the political affiliation of the Deep South, one that had begun forty years earlier as a segregationist backlash against the civil rights movement.

The extremists I had seen cheering for Barry Goldwater in 1964 were now firmly entrenched in power.

11

THE SUMMER OF BLINKING RED

Imagine that terrorists hijack four commercial jets, crash them into buildings, kill nearly three thousand Americans, and the government does not immediately launch an investigation.

People forget that the only reason we had an investigation into September 11, as flawed and incomplete as it was, is that the families of the victims demanded it. They demanded it for more than a year before they managed to overcome the president's resistance to opening up his government to scrutiny.

The September 11 families wanted an official account of what happened, how it happened, and why. Most Americans did.

In one of the few cases where the White House did not get its way, Congress mandated an investigation. To ensure political neutrality, the ten-member investigating committee would be led by a Republican chairman, former New Jersey governor

Thomas Kean, and a Democratic vice chairman, former Indiana congressman Lee Hamilton.

I followed their work closely and was perplexed by how determined the White House was to not cooperate; to not provide witnesses and documents, claiming a blanket protection of so-called executive privilege. The administration would not allow government officials to sit for interviews with the National Commission on Terrorist Attacks upon the United States unless an agency handler was at their side. These tactics did much to make the administration's reputation as one that is unusually insistent on circling the wagons and operating in secrecy. In my view, this noncooperation rose to a level that can only be called obstruction.

In a July 2003 interim report the commission complained that President Bush was resisting its investigation while publicly pledging good faith and cooperation. By October of that year, the commission resorted to issuing subpoenas for documents the Federal Aviation Administration had failed to produce. "What we have here is a very angry commission," Chairman Kean told *The Washington Post*. "This is a sign that we are not loath to use a subpoena on other agencies if we need to. . . . Hopefully this will tell other agencies that haven't complied with our requests to get on the stick and do so."

The FAA proffered its renewed good faith and offered up various excuses for not turning over the documents the commission had sought: it had overlooked them in its search process; the Department of Justice was reviewing the same documents to aid its prosecution of Zacarias Moussaoui, the so-called twentieth hijacker.

With the FAA compelled to act under subpoena, the foot-dragging continued at other agencies. By November, the commission was issuing subpoenas for relevant documents the Pentagon had withheld and was threatening to subpoena White House records as well.

"There is a clear message today to the White House and the C.I.A. and the rest of the agencies that we're dealing with," Commissioner Timothy J. Roemer told *The New York Times.*

A month later, in December, former senator Max Cleland resigned his seat on the commission in protest. He said publicly that President Bush and his government "knew a whole lot more about these terrorists before September 11 than it has ever admitted."

"They had a plan to go to war," he said, "and when nine-eleven happened that's what they did." The commission, underfunded and faced with an arbitrary deadline for reporting to the American people, lumbered on.

There were key questions I wanted answered down to the last detail, and if the White House was saying one thing while doing the opposite, I doubted my questions would be put to rest in any final report. The Department of Justice had refused to provide documents on Zacarias Moussaoui, whom the FBI had arrested on a visa violation in Minnesota that summer, on August 16, 2001. The FBI said it arrested him specifically to thwart a domestic terrorist attack it feared was in the planning stage. The FBI had identified Moussaoui as an Islamic extremist and a potential "suicide hijacker." A flight school instructor had alerted the FBI to the suspicious behavior of Moussaoui. The foreign student wanted to learn how to fly a Boeing 747 but had little background in even general aviation and professed no interest in becoming a commercial airline pilot. The FBI supervisor in Minneapolis complained about the lack of interest in the Moussaoui case at headquarters in Washington. The commission's final report gave this account:

"On September 4, the FBI sent a teletype to the CIA, the FAA, the Customs Service, the State Department, the INS and the Secret Service summarizing the known facts regarding Moussaoui. It did not report the case agent's personal assessment that Moussaoui planned to hijack an airplane. It did contain the FAA's comment that it was not unusual for Middle Easterners to attend flight training schools in the United States. Although the Minneapolis agents wanted to tell the FAA from the beginning about Moussaoui, FBI headquarters instructed Minneapolis that it could not share the more complete report the case agent had prepared for the FAA. The Minneapolis supervisor sent the case agent in person to the local FAA office to fill in what he thought were gaps in the FBI headquarters teletype. No FAA actions seem to have been taken in response. There was substantial disagreement between Minneapolis agents and FBI headquarters as to what Moussaoui was planning to do. In one conversation between a Minneapolis supervisor and a headquarters agent, the latter complained that Minneapolis's FISA request was couched in a manner intended to get people 'spun up.' The supervisor replied that was precisely his intent. He said he was 'trying to keep someone from taking a plane and crashing into the World Trade Center.'"

This was a week before terrorists did just that.

Director of Central Intelligence George Tenet was briefed on the FBI's arrest of Moussaoui within ten days. The CIA and the FBI were both in the loop, despite the "wall" between them that pro-administration witnesses kept blaming for the "inevitability" of the September 11 attacks.

The commission reported: "On August 23, DCI Tenet was briefed about the Moussaoui case in a briefing titled, 'Islamic Extremist Learns to Fly.' Tenet was also told that Moussaoui wanted to learn to fly a 747, paid for his training in cash, was interested to learn the doors do not open in flight, and wanted to fly a simulated flight from London to New York. He was told that the FBI had arrested Moussaoui because of a visa overstay and that the CIA was working the case with the FBI. Tenet told us that no connection to al Qaeda was apparent to him at the time."

No connection was apparent? How is that possible? I was irate to see the commission go away satisfied with that answer. *Tenet told us.* And the line of questioning ends there?

The commission showed the same infuriating lack of assertiveness on the so-called Phoenix memo, the e-mail that an FBI agent in Arizona sent up the chain of command two full months before September 11. He sent his e-mails to the radical fundamentalist unit and the bin Laden unit at FBI Headquarters in Washington, and to the bureau's field office in New York.

The agent reported that Islamic radicals were in the United States and enrolled in flight schools. In notifying the UBL unit, he had made at least a theoretical connection between al-Qaeda and the student pilots who had aroused his suspicion.

I wanted the commission to follow that thread until there were no facts left to report. Who read the agent's e-mails in Washington and New York? What did those officials say or do in response?

The FBI agent in Phoenix did his job. He reported what he knew through proper channels. The commission had a duty to document what happened between the moment the agent pressed the send button in Phoenix, on July 10, 2001, and the moment American Airlines Flight 11 crashed into the North Tower of the World Trade Center on September 11.

Instead, the Phoenix memo gets a half page of attention in the 567-page final report. The commission said no one in the three FBI offices looked at the Phoenix memo until after September 11.

There may be legitimate reasons why that happened. What were these reasons? Were the FBI agents in the radical fundamentalist and bin Laden units too busy tracking down other potential threats? Were they out of the office on sick leave? Away on vacation? Whether the facts were innocuous or damning, I wanted them. I was not content with "No managers at headquarters saw the memo before September 11, and the New York Field Office took no action."

The commission's last word on the matter was: "If the memo had been distributed in a timely fashion and its recommendations acted on promptly, we do not believe it would have uncovered the plot. It might well, however, have sensitized the FBI so that it might have taken the Moussaoui matter more seriously the next month."

Fair enough, but the commission strays too far into what might have happened without reporting what did in fact happen. We are left to wonder: Did someone who was paid to protect Americans from terrorists simply drop the ball? The commission never explains why it believed that September 11 would have happened just as it did even if the Phoenix memo had gotten all the attention it warranted in Washington and New York. What are the facts that support that belief?

When the commission issued its final report, after much stonewalling by the administration's witnesses, my questions were left unanswered.

The commission did do a magnificent job of re-creating the awful drama of September 11. The *Final Report of the National Commission on Terrorist Attacks upon the United States* became a bestseller. The minute-by-minute account of what happened on the four hijacked flights was riveting, if horrifying.

The commission focused extensively on how to reform law enforcement and domestic security, and that was just the cover the Congress needed. It would give the illusion of leadership. It is always politically risky to demand and work for accountability—you never know what you might uncover. But Congress is in its comfort zone when fiddling with new rules and mechanisms and minutiae. The Homeland Security Committee, led by senators Susan Collins and Joe Lieberman, held scores of hearings and embarked on a sweeping overhaul of agencies and procedures. It was all well and good, but it was a diversion of the attention that should have been focused on how the attacks had managed to succeed in the first place. There is political cover in diversions, and it pays dividends in the form of campaign bragging rights. Lawmakers who buried themselves in the bureaucratic overhaul were popping the buttons off their shirts with pride. That was so much safer than assuming the risk of exercising leadership on the questions that mattered.

As CIA director George Tenet would testify, "The system

was blinking red" in the summer of 2001, given the Phoenix memos and the capture of Moussaoui in Minneapolis. All levels of national security should have acted on these investigative breakthroughs generated by the agents in the field in Phoenix and Minneapolis. *They* deserved to have George W. Bush hang the Presidential Medal of Freedom around their necks, not the useless George Tenet.

I was perplexed to see the commission bow to preposterous preconditions on obtaining testimony from President Bush and Vice President Cheney: No testimony was to be given under oath; no recordings or official transcripts of their testimony were to be made; and they would only testify together—in the same room, at the same time. It was beyond belief that the commission did not insist on or publicly scold these two public servants for refusing to testify separately. Instead, the commission allowed itself to be bullied into accepting a White House demand that was tragic and even laughable at the same time: that the president of the United States would not consent to answer questions unless his vice president was seated at his elbow.

Further, the president and vice president barred the commission from studying the full text of the August 6, 2001, Presidential Daily Briefing entitled "Bin Laden Determined to Attack Inside the United States." Under questioning by Commissioner Richard Ben-Veniste, National Security Adviser Condoleezza Rice embarrassed herself by repeatedly refusing to say the ominous title of the August 2001 briefing. It was her job to track this threat. Incredibly, on September 11, 2001, she was scheduled to speak at the School of Advanced International Studies at Johns Hopkins University. At a time when the system was "blinking red," Rice was to deliver a speech on national security that did not even mention the threat of domestic attacks by al-Qaeda or Islamic extremism in general.

As the September 11 families sought facts and answers, the president and his administration were on a damage-control mission. They were out to duck blame, taking the position that the only adequate warning before September 11 would have been a memo that identified nineteen hijackers, four commercial flights, four airports, four targets, and the hour the men planned to board those flights. Only then would the system have been adequately blinking red.

Commissioner Jamie Gorelick had reminded Rice that the previous administration had warned President Bush that an attack inside the United States was imminent.

"A commission that was chartered by Bill Clinton and Newt Gingrich, two very different people covering pretty much the political spectrum, put together a terrific panel to study the issue of terrorism and report to the new administration as it began, and you took that briefing, I know," Gorelick said, as Rice sat stone-faced. "That commission said we are going to get hit in the United States and we are going to get hit big. That's number one. And number two, we have big systemic problems. The FBI doesn't work the way it should and it doesn't communicate with the intelligence communities. Now you have said to us that your policy review was meant to be comprehensive. You took your time because you wanted to get at the hard issues and have a hard-hitting comprehensive policy, and yet there is nothing in it about the vast domestic landscape that we were all warned needed so much attention. Can you give me the answer to the question: Why?"

The thrust of Rice's answer was that the president had been in office only 233 days. It was another way of saying his watch had not really started. Apparently her watch had not really started either.

With al-Qaeda about to attack, the national security adviser was focused on the theoretical threat of a long-range missile attack on the United States. That was the subject of her undelivered September 11 speech at Johns Hopkins.

In her answers to the commission, Rice kept steering the testimony back to the previous administration.

"I think the question is, why over all of these years did we not address the structural problems that were there, with the FBI, with the CIA . . ."

Rice is a brilliant academic and a policy wonk of the first order. She does not see the forest or the trees, but can talk for hours—in numbing detail—about the bark, the leaves, the branches, and the roots. That was what she did before the commission. She kept diverting attention from key issues and burying the record in monologues about the need for "structural reforms" in how the nation guards itself against terrorist attack. By definition, then, no one in the administration made a mistake on domestic security in the nine months leading up to September 11. The structure was wrong, not the people in charge of it—especially not National Security Adviser Condoleezza Rice.

"I just don't buy the argument that we weren't shaking the trees enough and that something was going to fall out that gave us somehow that little piece of information that would have led to connecting all of those dots," Rice told the commission.

She insisted that "the president of the United States had us at battle stations." But her subtext was: *if only a previous administration had put the right structural reforms in place.*

When Rice ran the clock on Commissioner Bob Kerrey, he practically begged her not to eat up his time, "I've got ten minutes. . . . Please don't filibuster me, it is not fair, it is not fair." Kerrey was so flustered at Rice wasting his time he kept calling her "Dr. Clarke," evidently confusing her name with a previous witness's, the former White House counterterrorism chief Richard A. Clarke. That was what people remembered about the exchange, that Rice had corrected Kerrey on his recurring gaffe about her name, not that he was zeroing in on key issues as his witness desperately played defense. This exchange was emblematic of the entire obstruction effort by the administration. He had ten minutes to get to the truth, and Rice was lulling the audience with long-winded talk about missile strikes versus long-range bombers and the regional "basing" needed to support long-range bombers.

"You're figuring this out, you've got to give a very long answer," Kerrey said. Rice kept talking over Kerrey as he grunted and groaned in exasperation.

Kerrey interrupted one of Rice's monologues with, "Dr. Clarke, look, let me say, I think if you had come in here and said, 'Look, we screwed up, we made a lot of mistakes.' You obviously don't want to use the 'M-word' in here, and I would say fine, it's game, set and match, I understand that. I mean, but this 'strategic' and 'tactical,' it sounds like something from a seminar."

I felt as Kerrey did: It was understandable, and even forgivable, that mistakes were made; however, it was crucial to identify mistakes *first*. Lamentably, Condoleezza Rice adamantly refused to identify mistakes and continually deflected attention away from herself and onto the Clinton administration.

National Security Adviser Rice was determined to keep the commission talking about the larger so-called war on terror and not expose the Bush administration to criticism over the failures leading up to September 11. It was obvious to me that she had been prepped by political handlers on how to use Kerrey's support for the Iraq War to deflect his line of questioning. Everyone in the room knew what was going on when Rice was able to quote a foreign policy speech Kerrey had given and to use his own views to undermine him while innocently claiming she admired those views.

There was a bit of laughter in the room when Rice said, with barely concealed insincerity, "I was blown away by the speech. This was a brilliant speech."

But Kerrey kept boring in on the lack of follow-up to the Phoenix memo and the Moussouai arrest.

"I don't need a catastrophic event to know that the CIA and the FBI don't do a very good job of communicating," he said. "All it had to do was go out on Intel link and the game is over. It ends. This conspiracy would have been rolled up."

Rice continued to burn through Kerrey's ten minutes by referring back to the previous administration.

"The restructuring of the FBI was not going to be done in the 233 days in which we were in office," she said.

Exasperated, Kerrey said, "Dr. Rice, everybody who does national security in this town knows the FBI and the CIA don't talk, so if you have a meeting on the fifth of July where you're trying to make certain that your domestic agencies are preparing a defense against a possible attack—you knew al-Quada cells were in the United States—you've got to follow-up! And my question is: What was your follow-up? What's the paper trail that shows that you and [White House chief of staff] Andy Card followed up from this meeting and made certain that the FBI and the CIA were talking?"

The silicon chip in Rice's head kept spooling out policy-speak and she did what she was sent to do—bury the relevant questions in an avalanche of tedium and run the clock on the most aggressive commissioners.

An urgent warning from the outgoing Democratic administration was not enough; only the "new Pearl Harbor" that the New American Century had talked about would put us properly on guard.

Rice told the commission, "The unfortunate—and I really do think it's extremely tragic—fact, is that sometimes until there is a catastrophic event that forces people to think differently, that forces people to overcome old customs and old culture and old fears about domestic intelligence and the relationship, that you don't get that kind of change."

I fault the Senate for allowing the investigation to come to an unsatisfying conclusion. It had the power to insist on accountability but stayed in its comfort zone, enacting a gigantic reshuffling of federal agencies, a reorganization that would quickly prove ineffectual when Hurricane Katrina swept through New Orleans.

I pass no judgment on the infinite number of conspiracy theories that grew out of September 11, but will say only that the commission invited wild speculation when it allowed itself to effectively be bullied by the White House into releasing a "final" report based on an obviously incomplete investigation. The final report, as dramatic and riveting as it is, left key questions unanswered and invited Americans to fill in the blanks on their own.

In my view, the 9/11 commissioners relied too heavily on their sixty-member staff. Any busy person who has served on a national or local commission knows that the paid staff has the tiller in hand; the inquiry goes where they steer it.

Finally, I was distressed to see an administration insider and Bush campaign aide, Philip Zelikow, appointed to serve as executive director of the investigation. The staff reported to him; all materials crossed his desk before getting to the commissioners. Zelikow had worked with Condoleezza Rice on national security issues. Now he was heading an investigation in which Rice would be under scrutiny for actions she took or failed to take as national security adviser to President Bush, in that summer of 2001 when "the system was blinking red."

In 1997, Zelikow and Secretary Rice coauthored a book on the reunification of Germany. Soon after the commission disbanded, Rice hired Zelikow as her counselor at the State Department.

Zelikow, a brilliant academic who has worked at Harvard and other respected institutions, once coedited a book entitled *Why People Don't Trust Government.* Part of the answer certainly must be that government insiders are sometimes appointed to manage investigations into government behavior.

12

IN CYCLE

My political fortunes were sealed in the wee hours of November 3, 2004, when Ohio's twenty electoral votes went to President George W. Bush, electing him to a second term. I knew then that my own reelection bid two years hence was in jeopardy—we would still be at war in Iraq, Rhode Islanders would still be furious with the president, and I would be the lead Republican on the ballot. It would not matter that I had opposed the president on many of his policies. The voters would get at him by going through me.

Every two years a third of the Senate is up for reelection, or "in cycle," but of those thirty-three or thirty-four seats, only seven or eight are really in play. Many seats are safe, and the power of the incumbency makes many elections a formality.

My seat was not one of those. I would definitely be in play in 2006, in a primary as well as the general election. When a senator's term is in cycle, he or she has to devote enormous energy to fund-raising, the least interesting and most unpleasant aspect of holding office. Even in the best of circumstances, it is daunting to raise the millions required to be a competitive candidate for the Senate. Doing the work of the Senate and being an attentive parent and spouse is exponentially more demanding when you have to get serious about chasing campaign dollars. Raising money is harder still when you happen to be a Rockefeller Republican who is pro-choice, pro-environment, antiwar, and fiscally responsible.

Every "Rockefeller" vote I cast in 2005 and 2006 had a chilling effect on the Republican base that I needed to help finance my campaign. Further compounding my problems, every one of my votes in favor of the president's federal judges, non-lifetime appointees, as well as a host of other votes I had cast, turned off the independent and Democratic voters I needed to support me in 2006.

The campaign climate had changed radically from 2000 when there actually were some pro-choice, pro-environment Republican donors willing to believe the party might change. Five years later, these former supporters of mine were disgusted with the Bush legacy and reluctant to see their names associated with it. They stopped giving.

On top of the president's reelection in 2004, Senate Republicans built their numbers to a robust 55-to-45 majority. With these strong numbers, my fellow Republicans could afford to marginalize me within my own caucus. Human nature being what it is, the leadership might want to exercise retribution for my wayward votes. In that event, could I even be effective representing Rhode Island in 2005 and 2006?

I was well aware of my options. I could decide not to run for reelection, as Illinois's senator Peter Fitzgerald chose to do in 2004 and Senator Mark Dayton of Minnesota had announced he would do in 2006. Alternatively, I could run as an independent. Or, I could even take the drastic step to switch parties as Democratic senators Ben Nighthorse Campbell and Richard Shelby had done in previous years. As I pondered the next two years, I knew that two bills extremely important to Rhode Island were scheduled for votes: the military Base Realignment and Closure bill (BRAC) and the six-year federal highway funding bill. Rhode Island has thousands of good-paying defense jobs, mainly in and around Newport. If I bolted the party, the White House and the Republican leadership would certainly target Rhode Island for heavy cuts, especially since the other three members of our state's congressional delegation were all Democrats. They would take their anger with me out on a million Rhode Islanders.

My dilemma was the same on the highway reauthorization, which allocates hundreds of billions of dollars for surface transportation projects across the country, raised mainly through the federal gasoline tax. As a member of the Environment and Public Works Committee, I was in a key position to protect the lucrative formula that brings Rhode Island a net gain of federal tax dollars. Could I jeopardize that by leaving the Republican Party?

I considered that course—not just to save my political skin, but because my moderate-to-liberal voting record would leave me with little influence in the Republican Party in a second Bush term. I was still assessing this bleak outlook a few days after the 2004 election when I returned to my home in McLean, Virginia. The phone rang. Was it the Democratic leadership trolling for out-of-favor Republicans who were thinking of finding a new home? It was Senate Majority Whip Mitch McConnell of Kentucky. Senator McConnell had always treated me well, though we usually disagreed on the issues. I counted him a gentleman and a friend.

He said, "Linc, I know what you must be thinking, but we need you in the Republican Party."

I was stunned. Was Mitch McConnell a mind reader?

"We respect your voice in the caucus, and we like you," he said. "We'll help you in your reelection bid."

I thought Republicans would be busy reveling in the conservative victory. Instead, the leadership reached out to me at a time when I was genuinely assessing whether I needed to set a new course for myself in order to better serve my state, my country, and my personal political future.

It was still a fact of life that my reelection prospects in two years were dim, given the "R" after my name. But that unexpected call from Senator McConnell buoyed my competitive spirit. It was an important reason why I decided to remain a Republican.

Senator McConnell backed up word with deed over the next two years. Not only did Rhode Island prosper through the highway reauthorization bill, but, while many states were losing military jobs through BRAC, Rhode Island was one of the few that had a net gain.

There was no call from Democrats the week after the election. I can only guess they were so stunned at our four-seat gain in the Senate they were too demoralized to even try to a hook a potential defector. Only Mitch McConnell was on the job that day, while Republicans partied and Democrats sank into gloom.

13

THE KITCHEN TEST

When President Bush won reelection in 2004, he famously declared, "Let me put it to you this way: I earned capital in this campaign, political capital, and now I intend to spend it." I knew that one result of this arrogance would be that we would see more polarizing figures nominated to join the administration in its second term. The president was inclined to put right-wing firebrands in positions of power. Without doubt, John Bolton was the most divisive personality he nominated. A supporter of the Project for the New American Century, Bolton was deputy secretary of state for arms control when the president nominated him as our next ambassador to the United Nations. Bolton was a fierce critic of the United Nations and, in fact, had expressed contempt for the world body. Nonetheless, President Bush asked us to grant Bolton the nation's highest diplomatic credentials.

In sending up the Bolton nomination, the president was thumbing his nose at his political opponents and even our allies, and I sensed his glee. That was his message to the Senate: *Get used to it. John Bolton is America's top diplomat at the United Nations.*

The Bolton nomination was a needless fight, but the president was determined to have it. I had opposed the president on many issues, but there was one principle I tried to uphold consistently, one I had believed in as a city councilman and mayor: An executive should have the freedom to choose the people who serve him in important positions of responsibility. Lawmakers should give the executive leeway when exercising their power to advise and consent on such appointments. They should not unreasonably interfere with the executive's power to assemble his own team. On that basis, I had supported nominations that I thought were ill-advised: John Ashcroft as attorney general; Gale Norton as interior secretary; and Condolezzza Rice to replace Colin Powell as secretary of state. I made an exception to my noninterference rule whenever we considered lifetime appointments to the judiciary. But when an appointee would serve only for the term of the executive, I wanted to let the executive have his first choice.

In 2006, I had a primary opponent from the extreme right, and he criticized me for fighting the president on the tax cut, the war, and other issues. I defended myself to Rhode Island Republicans by stressing that I had consistently supported the president's non-lifetime appointments.

Now, with the Bolton nomination, the administration put me in an impossible bind. Bolton was the antidiplomat. He had no talent for working with people who disagreed with him, let alone working on our most difficult and sensitive international issues. We all know the United Nations is imperfect, but we need the framework it provides for a discussion among the family of nations. Common sense tells you that a sour personality with contempt for the organization will be less than effective there.

In April 2005, the Senate Foreign Relations Committee met to hear testimony from the nominee. I was the third-ranking Republican on the panel, after Chairman Richard Lugar and Senator Chuck Hagel. That put me fifth in line to question Bolton, factoring in senators Joe Biden and Paul Sarbanes, the two highest-ranking Democrats.

Many supporters and detractors wanted to witness Bolton's testimony, so we met in the larger of two rooms available to us, a cavernous hall in the Hart Senate Office Building.

John Bolton, though personally unsuited for the diplomatic corps, certainly comes with credentials that qualify him in all other respects. He is a Yale graduate and, undoubtedly, a smart man. He cultivates an interesting persona, too, with the bushy mustache, wire-rim glasses, and perhaps the longest haircut in Foggy Bottom. He sat alone at the witness table, glowering as he waited for the hearing to begin. He knew the Democrats had the long knives out for him. He also knew he had the votes to win a favorable recommendation to the full Senate, and I thought that probably burned him up more than anything else; he wanted to get his vote and move on, but the Washington process required him to sit for the C-SPAN cameras and let the Democrats draw blood.

We all knew that Under Secretary Bolton had the votes because just about everything in Washington happens according to a script. Chairman Richard Lugar knew that every Democrat would vote against Bolton and every Republican would vote for him. The count would be ten to eight and the nomination would go to the full Senate with a favorable recommendation.

In his opening statement, Mr. Bolton said that Kofi Annan, the Ghanaian secretary-general of the United Nations, had phoned him when he heard of his nomination as U.S. ambassador. Mr. Bolton meant to imply that the secretary-general supported his nomination, but he never said it explicitly. That piqued my curiosity. When it was my turn to question him, I asked point-blank whether Kofi Annan had endorsed him. The nominee seemed surprised that someone on the committee had paid any attention to his opening statement. Interest groups in Washington were surely parsing every word, but opening statements tend to fade into the background noise on Capitol Hill. Mr. Bolton stammered a bit when he described the phone call from the secretary-general in a little more detail: "He said—well, I probably shouldn't get into it—but he said, 'Get yourself confirmed quickly.' "

That left me to muse: *Then why leave that out of your opening statement?*

We covered some ground on Taiwan and the People's Republic of China, then I focused on a speech Mr. Bolton had given two years earlier in Seoul, South Korea, at a particularly delicate time in the Six-Party Talks, an effort by the United States, China, Russia, Japan, and South Korea to negotiate an end to nuclear weapons development in North Korea.

Bolton had used needlessly provocative and insulting language in that speech, which he delivered on July 31, 2003. President Bush had declared "Mission Accomplished" in Iraq a few weeks earlier, and Bolton, it seems, was ready to take on North Korea next.

In a warlike speech delivered at the Seoul Hilton, Mr. Bolton invoked Kim Jong Il's name forty-one times, slamming the dictator, the tyrant, the blackmailer, the extortionist. It was unnecessarily personal and infinitely undiplomatic, coming as it did on the eve of these important arms-control talks. We would alienate not only our adversary but our allies in those talks.

Predictably, the North Koreans reacted with name-calling of their own. They called Bolton "rude human scum" and "a beastly man bereft of reason."

Going into the hearing, my mindset was that the Bolton tirade in Seoul disqualified him for his current job as under secretary of state for arms control, let alone a promotion to U.S. ambassador to the United Nations. But I was prepared to listen to his side of the story, and even to be persuaded by it.

Our lead negotiator in the Six-Party Talks was Jack Pritchard, a career army officer who had worked for Republican and Democratic administrations and was an accomplished, veteran negotiator. He tried to assuage the North Koreans' anger and keep the talks on track. Word leaked out that Mr. Pritchard had told the North Koreans to ignore the provocation from Seoul, that Mr. Bolton did not represent the official U.S. position. That, in turn, caught the attention of Republican Senator Jon Kyl of Arizona, and he set out to score a point for the hardliners on North Korea.

Senator Kyl fired off a letter to Mr. Pritchard's boss, Secretary of State Colin Powell, demanding that he weigh in and clarify who speaks for U.S. policy. This was a key moment in our diplomatic efforts at the Six-Party Talks. Who speaks for American foreign policy: the savvy, cool negotiator Jack Pritchard or the hot-tempered clashist John Bolton? To my dismay, Secretary Powell supported Bolton and cut loose his own man in the field. He wrote back to Senator Kyl to affirm that Mr. Bolton had gotten it right; the Seoul speech had been cleared by the State Department and was consistent with Bush administration policy.

Powell also announced, in the letter to Kyl, that Jack Pritchard would be leaving the State Department and the talks. He had resigned.

China, our principal ally in the talks, was furious at how Bolton had undermined the arms-control effort. As North Korea's primary source of food and fuel, the Chinese had immense leverage over Kim Jong Il, and we knew we needed China with us if we were serious about disarming North Korea peacefully.

By September, top Chinese diplomats were complaining that the United States did not have a negotiating strategy in the international drive to keep deliverable nuclear weapons out of Kim Jong Il's hands. China's vice foreign minister, Wang Yi, called the United States the "main obstacle" to progress at the talks.

This was the context of my question to John Bolton a year and a half later, at his confirmation hearing. I wanted to know what he was trying to accomplish by publicly humiliating Kim Jong Il in Seoul.

In his answer he denied that he had hurt our arms-control efforts on the Korean peninsula and went on to say, "I can tell you what our ambassador to South Korea, Tom Hubbard, said after the speech. He said, 'Thanks a lot for that speech, John; it will help us a lot out here.'"

Ambassador Hubbard, who had left South Korea in 2004, called my office the next day and starkly contradicted Mr. Bolton's testimony. He said he had strongly objected to the speech.

This really tested my self-imposed rule on presidential appointments, that I would always support the president's right to have the nominee of his choice in a non-lifetime appointment. If Bolton had knowingly given a false answer to my question in committee, he had lost my vote. Many Republicans reveled in the 1998 impeachment of President Bill Clinton on a perjury charge; now, if Mr. Bolton had lied to me under oath, I would have no problem going back to my Republican base in Rhode Island and defending my nay vote at the many political breakfasts and spaghetti suppers I loyally attended.

Over the next few days, things began to change. As Ambassador Hubbard worked with my staff to clarify his exact recollections, words were parsed into finer and finer shades of meaning and soon I was not certain that Bolton had misled me. Under my own rule, I would have to vote to seat him. At the president's prerogative, the most undiplomatic man I had met in Washington was going to be our top diplomat at the United Nations. What glee that must have given the White House honchos who had rushed to John Bolton's defense in the aftermath of the hearing.

I was extraordinarily frustrated with the way our chairman, Senator Richard Lugar of Indiana, handled the Bolton nomination. Senator Lugar came to the Senate in 1977, the same year as my father, and devoted his entire career to international relations. He sacrificed opportunities to move to the Appropriations and Finance Committees, assignments that arguably have more power than the Foreign Relations Committee. Inasmuch as he was devoted to international affairs, it had to gall him to see President Bush and Vice President Cheney undoing decades of work that leaders of both parties had achieved in building and strengthening international institutions. Time and again, Senator Lugar showed an unwillingness to fight with the White House over the direction of our foreign policy. The John Bolton nomination was the signature moment, the crowning event, that demonstrated the White House's contempt for Congress. It directly challenged everything Senator Lugar had stood for over his long career. At this critical time, the chairman needed to have a quiet visit with the president and impose a few ground rules of his own. On this controversial nomination, Senator Lugar needed to say, *Mr. President, do what you will, but John Bolton is not going to the United Nations on my watch.*

Senator Lugar needed to make it clear that he expected to be consulted, that a Rhodes scholar and a lifelong expert on foreign affairs was not about to take orders from an extreme fringe of U.N.-haters on Pennsylvania Avenue.

Like Chairman Lugar, Secretary Powell must have been horrified by what the hard-liners in the administration were doing, but he knuckled under and told Senator Kyl what he wanted to hear: John Bolton was right and Jack Pritchard was wrong. Secretary Powell must have known the Chinese would be incensed to see the Six-Party Talks set back by the loss of the American special envoy. Ever the good soldier, Powell saluted and did what the commander in chief wanted done. I was saddened to see the secretary weigh in against a fellow soldier, Jack Pritchard, and support Mr. Bolton.

When I finished questioning Mr. Bolton at the hearing, a protester in the back of the room shouted, "No to Bolton! Yes to the U.N.! No to Bolton! Yes to the U.N." Capitol Police surrounded the protester and muscled him out as Chairman Lugar tapped the gavel, almost inaudibly calling for order. When the last echoes of the protester's shouts receded in the marble corridors, Chairman Lugar, seemingly oblivious to the high emotions incited by this nomination, intoned, "I now call upon the distinguished senator from Connecticut, Senator Dodd."

Before the hearing concluded, we heard some colorful testimony from Carl Ford, a former State Department colleague of Bolton's, who described him as "a quintessential kiss-up, kick-down sort of guy. There are a lot of them around here. I'm sure you've met them. But the fact is that he stands out; that he's got a bigger kick. And it gets bigger and stronger the further down the bureaucracy he is kicking."

Nine days later, on April 20, 2005, we met to carve the fait accompli in stone, a ten-to-eight vote that would send the Bolton nomination to the Senate floor with a favorable recommendation. Senator Christopher Dodd, a natural orator, was in full battle cry that day. His booming voice has a natural volume even when he is not trying to be heard a block away. Senator Dodd's statement urging a nay vote on Bolton was devastating. He held up a State Department organizational chart showing where Bolton figured in as under secretary for arms control. A red arrow zigzagged down through the chart and pointed to an obscure analyst at the bottom of the hierarchy. Bolton was not happy with a report the analyst had written, so he left his lofty office and made his way down into the bowels of the building to berate the man in front of his colleagues.

Opponents meant to show that Mr. Bolton's temperament was all wrong for an ambassador: he was mean-spirited, vindictive, and resentful of unvarnished and frank analysis that did not conform to the party line.

As Mr. Ford had testified, Bolton would lash out whenever some State Department underling failed to spin a report the way the head office wanted it spun. That mind-set, working toward a predetermined outcome, was pervasive in the Bush administration, as senators in both parties well knew.

In a thunderous voice, Dodd excoriated Mr. Bolton for his abuse of lowly subordinates. It was political theater because we all knew the president had the favorable votes he needed for Mr. Bolton in the Foreign Relations Committee.

When testimony concluded, Chairman Lugar, doing the president's bidding, confidently called the roll.

I voted yea for Mr. Bolton, and immediately thought, *I've been proud to cast thousands of votes in the Senate. This is one time I'm not.*

The roll call continued toward the preordained outcome, every Republican in favor, every Democrat opposed. Then Republican senator George Voinovich stopped everything in the room when he said, "I can't vote for this man."

We all looked at the senator from Ohio. *Did he just say he's voting no?*

I was a rookie senator, but I knew that surprises like this almost never happen.

Senator Voinovich apologized for not having followed the John Bolton saga as closely as he might have in the weeks preceding the vote now being called.

"I've heard enough today that I don't feel comfortable about voting for Mr. Bolton," he said. The president's man had failed "the kitchen test," the commonsense test the senator's mother would apply when sizing up a person's character or behavior.

Is this someone you would like to have at your kitchen table?

The Bolton nomination, once certain, would fail on a tie vote in committee. Chairman Lugar inexplicably allowed the roll call to continue. He had lost control of the script and had no idea what else to do.

The clerk repeated each name and each vote, as if this were business as usual: *Feingold of Wisconsin, Nay . . . Alexander of Tennessee, Yea . . . Boxer of California, Nay . . .*

Finally, Joe Biden, the ranking Democrat on the committee, interrupted Chairman Lugar's robotic performance. The two senators had served together on the committee for thirty years, and I thought that history probably trumped any partisan pleasure Senator Biden might otherwise have taken in our chairman's predicament. He said, simply, "Dick, you're going to lose this vote. I think you want to change course."

The roll call stopped, and after a brief huddle Senator Lugar was forced to send the Bolton nomination to the full Senate with no recommendation. And there it languished.

Frustrated in defeat, the president waited until Congress left Washington for the August recess and invoked his power to appoint John Bolton unilaterally as ambassador to the United Nations. The Constitution gives the president "power to fill up all vacancies that may happen during the recess of the Senate by granting commissions which shall expire at the end of their next session." That meant the president needed to come back to the Senate if he wanted Bolton to serve beyond the end of the 109th Congress and through the 110th, when his second term as president would end.

He wanted it that way. It was not long before we were back dealing with the Bolton nomination, this time in the summer of 2006. With renewed determination, the White House pushed us to seat Bolton through an affirmative vote in the Senate. To that end, the administration wooed Senator Voinovich, and in the fall of 2006 he had a change of heart on the kitchen test. He agreed to reverse course and support the Bolton nomination.

Chairman Lugar scheduled a vote for the last meeting before I faced a far-right opponent in the Rhode Island Republican Senate primary. GOP strategists were betting I would vote for Bolton to defuse that issue in my primary.

I told Chairman Lugar I considered my first vote a mistake and was determined not to make the same mistake twice. I said I would break my own long-held rule on presidential nominations. In these extraordinary circumstances, I would apply the kitchen test in Senator Voinovich's stead and the Bolton nomination would fail again in committee.

Enough was enough. After a year of Bolton-style leadership in New York, we had a record to go by now. I was determined not to leave our U.N. mission in the hands of a hostile personality with no talent for diplomacy.

Chairman Lugar postponed the vote indefinitely and the president dropped the nomination. John Bolton's tenure at the United Nations was over.

14

STACKING THE COURT

When President Bush triumphed in Ohio in 2004 and won a second term, it became likely that he would nominate one or more Supreme Court justices before leaving office. During the campaign, he said publicly he wanted to appoint justices who would vote with Clarence Thomas and Antonin Scalia. I could only imagine what some of the moderate justices must have been thinking during the first Bush term. Having worked to reconcile contentious issues related to freedom of speech, the right to privacy, and the separation of church and state, could they retire in good conscience and turn their seats over to justices who would immediately start to undo their decades of work?

During the president's first term, Democrats and Republicans in the Senate skirmished over his lower-court nominations and the tactics involved in staging a filibuster or breaking one. We all knew it was a warm-up for a Supreme Court fight, should a vacancy occur. It takes sixty votes to end a filibuster and invoke cloture, as the parliamentarians say. From 2000 to 2004 Democratic senators were able to exercise that sixty-vote rule to keep judges from the extreme right off the federal bench. Republicans constantly threatened to change the Senate rules to forbid the filibustering of judicial nominees. Senator Trent Lott called the rule change "the nuclear option" because it would set off a white flash of partisan fury and bring all business to a halt in an instant. It would change everything. The Democrats warned that if Republicans tampered with this long-honored right of the minority, they would shut down the Senate themselves. If that were to happen, the House might as well adjourn. The entire Congress, indeed the federal government itself, would be out of business until Republicans and Democrats made peace. Majority Leader Bill Frist scheduled a vote on the rule change for May 24, 2005, to show that he was serious.

To defuse the nuclear option, I joined what the press called the Gang of Fourteen, seven Republicans and seven Democrats who united to prevent the Republican leadership from resorting to mutual assured destruction.

In a Senate where Republicans outnumbered Democrats fifty-five to forty-five, virtually every nominee sent up by President Bush would get the fifty-one votes needed in a filibuster-proof world. Our Gang of Fourteen proposed a compromise: We seven Republicans would vote against the rule change and Democrats would agree not to filibuster GOP nominees to the bench unless "extraordinary circumstances" existed.

Senator John McCain was instrumental in the effort to craft a workable peace among senators. He knew that many Republicans wanted to avoid this showdown but did not want to buck the leadership. They would be delighted if Senator McCain and six others stood up and resisted. Assuming that all Democratic votes would hold against the nuclear option, it would take six Republican votes to make the difference in a 55–45 Senate. The senior senator from Arizona called us together in his office to work out an agreement that would stop the nuclear option. Early on, we had just five Republican senators who were willing to make that commitment: Olympia Snowe and Susan Collins, both of Maine, John Warner of Virginia, John McCain, and me. McCain was fast friends with Mike DeWine of Ohio and Lindsey Graham of South Carolina, and he skillfully brought them both into the peace talks. That made seven. We had our six, and one for insurance.

Mike DeWine and Lindsey Graham pressed for the "extraordinary circumstances" language that would keep the Democrats from filibustering the president's nominees as a matter of course. We all knew there was room to argue over what was extraordinary and what was not, but both sides could claim victory for now and we would have that fight another day.

We reached agreement on May 23, 2005, and when Leader Frist arrived at the Capitol the next morning, he did not have the votes to change the filibuster rule. Knowing it would fail, he took it off the calendar.

Our Gang of Fourteen had showed that, even in this polarized environment, seven Democrats and seven Republicans could band together to get something done for the good of the country. It was a rare feeling.

I think all fourteen of us felt that it was a very special

group we had formed. We had such veterans as Robert C. Byrd of West Virginia, Dan Inouye of Hawaii, and John Warner. Mark Pryor of Arkansas, Ken Salazar of Colorado, Ben Nelson of Nebraska, Lindsey Graham, and I were the first-term senators in the mix. We had pro-life Democrats and pro-choice Republicans. A diverse group had proved that government could work even if the White House was busy sowing division.

On July 1, 2005, six months after President Bush was inaugurated to a second term, Justice Sandra Day O'Connor announced that she would leave the court to spend more time with her ailing husband. I had always admired Justice O'Connor, as much for who she is as how she ruled. She had grown up on a hardscrabble ranch in Arizona and knew her way around cattle and livestock. She graduated from Stanford University at a time when few women went to college, let alone the very best colleges. She became a lawyer, served as Arizona's Senate majority leader, and rose to the United States Supreme Court upon her nomination by President Reagan. She provided wise counsel on the High Court, a voice of reason navigating complex issues and crafting opinions of sound legal and social judgment. Those qualities were most notably evident in *Stenberg v. Carhart,* the historic, if short-lived, five-to-four compromise that gave states the power to restrict abortion as long as they made an exception for the health of the mother.

I had seen firsthand how this divisive and highly emotional abortion issue could literally take over a debate focused on something else entirely. In 1985, my home state convened a constitutional convention to reform and improve Rhode Island government from top to bottom. It was my first elective office. Abortion quickly became the central issue. A majority of my fellow delegates voted to prohibit abortion in Rhode Island. It was all for naught, given that *Roe v. Wade* was the law of the land; but reason had no place in the debate. Our convention met at the State House in Providence, the most beautiful state capitol in America. One of our hundred delegates, Larry Dolan of Pawtucket, got down on his knees in the House chamber, clasped his hands, and beseeched us: *Save the babies! Save the babies!*

Justice O'Connor had proved her mettle in this sort of environment.

When Justice O'Connor stepped down, we all knew the Court could reverse course in future abortion cases and strike down the exception for the health of the mother. Indeed, many five-to-four decisions would be readdressed and overturned with a Bush nominee on the Court. Many Republicans relished that day; I was one of the few who dreaded it.

The president nominated John Roberts to the O'Connor seat, but before we could hear testimony, Chief Justice William Rehnquist lost his fight with cancer. That created a second vacancy on the Court. The president then wanted John Roberts to lead the Court as chief justice. He was quickly confirmed. Many Democrats thought they could replace one conservative with another without altering the delicate five-to-four balance on the court. I agreed.

It was another matter entirely when the president asked us to elevate a second conservative, Samuel Alito, to replace the moderate O'Connor. Given what the president had said about his desire to seat additional justices in the mold of Thomas and Scalia, I had grave concerns about Judge Alito. I was willing to give him a fair hearing.

In 2005, the administration hired former senator Dan Coats of Indiana, a Washington lawyer, to guide the nominee through a round of private meetings with senators. Often, these meetings would be shoehorned in between hearings, votes, and floor debates in the busy schedules we all kept. That was the case when Coats ushered Alito into an anteroom off the Senate chamber, where we could speak.

Senator Coats and Judge Alito had a press scrum on their heels, dozens of reporters and photographers elbowing for an angle and calling out questions. I had two of my staff members with me, Kevin Mathis and Chris Spina. The door closed, leaving the press corps outside, and for a moment it was just the five of us.

It seemed the wrong setting for what I wanted to say to Judge Alito. I wanted our meeting to stand out from the many others he would have with members who were not solid yea votes. In years to come, when he would be interpreting the Constitution in ways that would affect how Americans would live and the degree of liberty they would enjoy, I hoped he might remember what a freedom-loving Rhode Islander had said to him.

After a few words of small talk, I stood and said, "Judge Alito, let's have our conversation on the Senate steps." Senator Coats flashed a look of alarm. His eyes opened wide and he put his hands on me and tried to block the door. It was his job to make sure these scripted meetings went according to plan.

I physically moved Senator Coats out of my way, opened the door, and Judge Alito and I walked past some very surprised reporters, who had sat down on the floor, expecting a long wait. A few steps more and we disappeared into the passageway behind the Senate rostrum where they were barred from following.

From there, we walked out onto the Senate steps and looked across the Capitol lawn and First Street at the marble columns of the Supreme Court.

The nominee's body language, drawing up to his full height and leaning his head back as he did, said to me: *I know. You're not going to vote for me.*

I talked about the era in which we had both come of age, when abuses of executive power tested our faith in the government and the Vietnam War tore the country apart before our eyes.

"It's happening again," I said. "And it's getting worse every day. I hope you'll always think about the broader context of your decisions, not just how the argument looks on paper. You can choose to divide the country or heal it. Don't forget, you're taking Sandra Day O'Connor's seat."

Politically, the judge could take my advice or leave it. He knew he had the votes to win confirmation and take his seat in the magnificent building across the way. Most Republican members of the Gang of Fourteen agreed that Judge Alito did not meet the "extraordinary circumstances" threshold in the agreement. That meant Democrats did not have the votes to filibuster him. Some hotheads, oblivious to the political mathematics, wanted to filibuster him. That would have invited the nuclear option, and in the end we could get Judge Alito anyway, by a simple majority vote. In the midst of this Democratic disarray, their defeated presidential candidate, Senator

John Kerry of Massachusetts, made things worse by insisting on a filibuster that was doomed to failure by every headcount, even his own. Senator Kerry made his filibuster pronouncements from Davos, Switzerland, a playground of the rich and famous, where he was attending the World Economic Forum. That provided some irresistible red meat for the Republican base, an image of Senator Kerry in the Alps, saying *merci* and *bon soir* and sipping fancy wines while making a futile attempt to obstruct Judge Alito. Even the Democratic leadership was rankled.

I had deep misgivings about the judge, but I had done the math. I would vote against his appointment but would do nothing to invite the nuclear option. Ultimately, I voted with 52 Republicans and 19 Democrats to oppose a filibuster. And then I voted against seating the judge on the U.S. Supreme Court.

After reading his decisions on the Court of Appeals and studying his testimony in the Judiciary Committee, I opposed Judge Alito on three counts: I feared he would not respect a woman's constitutional right to privacy as it concerns her own body; that he would not uphold the commerce clause as the constitutional basis for much of our environmental protection laws; and that he would vote to expand executive powers at every opportunity. I had cast the only Republican vote against the war in Iraq, and now I voted against seating Samuel Alito. That made for considerable political trouble for me back home in Rhode Island, where I was facing a primary in the fall. My offices in Providence and Washington were bombarded with critical mail and phone calls from Rhode Island Republicans and Italian Americans of both parties.

Before the roll call, I thought I had Senator Olympia Snowe of Maine with me in opposing Judge Alito. There are perhaps six Republican senators who call themselves pro-choice, but it was publicly known that only Senator Snowe and I were likely to vote against him. After the party-line vote on the nomination in the Judiciary Committee, senators revealed in random press conferences and interviews whether they would vote for or against confirmation. The press was after me to disclose how I would vote, as they sought to tally the numbers and predict the outcome. They started to label me indecisive on this issue. It was easy, of course, for Democrats to announce opposition and for Republicans to announce support. That was not news. But I was a Republican vote to oppose Judge Alito and I was hoping for company from Olympia. On the Friday after the committee vote, she asked me to hold off on my announcement until Monday. She wanted to meet one last time with her Republican strategists over the weekend before announcing her opposition. I said, *That's fine. Let them call me indecisive until then.*

That Sunday evening, around eight o'clock, the phone rang at my home in Exeter, Rhode Island. On the first ring, I thought, *Olympia's voting for Alito.*

I picked up the receiver and Olympia was on the line. She said the Republican Party in Maine had vowed to field a challenger against her in a primary election if she opposed Alito.

A primary always invites a stronger challenger in the general election; this is an unavoidable dynamic that every incumbent politician has to confront. Could Senator Snowe afford to vote her conscience on the threat to *Roe v. Wade* and women's reproductive freedoms if it meant a costly and bitter fight in a primary? She would spend much of her campaign funds to combat negative advertising in that intraparty battle. Her Democratic opponent in the general election would gain advantage either way; she would lose the primary or go into the November election weakened.

Olympia had an excruciating decision to make. She made it, then called me to break the news.

In fairness to Olympia, her vote would not have mattered; Judge Alito had more than enough votes to win confirmation, including some from Democrats.

I already had an announced primary opponent; Olympia would be inviting one. Moreover, Rhode Island, unlike Maine, has an open primary system. Independent or unaffiliated voters could come out and vote for me in the Republican primary. My vote against Judge Alito might actually energize my primary campaign by attracting independent voters to my side. But, in Maine's closed-primary system, Olympia would be at the mercy of the Republican base.

In the end, Olympia had no primary in 2006. Because she was strong and well financed, the Democrats declined to actively engage her. She coasted to victory in a year that was abysmal for Republicans, and an utter rout in the Northeast.

Finally, as supporters of *Roe v. Wade* had feared, once Justice Alito was seated, the Supreme Court reversed course and upheld a 2003 federal abortion law that did not include an exception for the health of the mother. It had not taken the Court long to trample on the legacy of Justice Sandra Day O'Connor.

15

TRUMAN'S EAGLE

In December of 2004, I went to Iraq again, this time with senators Joseph Biden, Chuck Hagel, and Dianne Feinstein.

A little over a year had passed since my first visit. We stopped in Amman, Jordan, then flew east in a C-130 transport over arid brown terrain that seemed to stretch on without end. About an hour into the flight, as I looked out a porthole window, I saw a little greenery below as we approached Mesopotamia, in the valleys of the Tigris and Euphrates rivers. Over the Iraqi capital, we did a rapid, corkscrew descent into Camp Freedom, the American base at Baghdad Airport. There we donned flak jackets and climbed aboard Black Hawk helicopters for a flight to a base outside Fallujah, where fierce fighting had recently been a daily reality for our soldiers and marines. As a defensive tactic, the helicopters flew low and fast, to minimize our exposure to ground fire. We raced along the deck, climbing only to jump high-tension wires and other obstacles. A man who wanted to hit us with an assault rifle or a rocket-propelled grenade would need a lot of luck, not just skill. At low altitude and extreme speed we were suddenly in one place and then suddenly gone. Many times we scattered livestock, sheep, chickens, cows, goats, and I saw the faces of angry Iraqis looking up at us. Grateful as I was to the pilot, I wondered how we might win the heart and mind of a man who had to spend all day tracking down his livelihood after we passed.

We were briefed by military commanders in Fallujah, then flew back to Baghdad and the fortified Green Zone. Everything had changed from that visit the year before. Security was much tighter. We were unable to travel the ten-mile road between the airport and the Green Zone because the risk of being attacked with an improvised explosive device was too great. After almost twenty months of combat, the reality of Iraq was that the mightiest military force on earth had not been able to secure the most vital ten miles of road in the country.

I asked our military escorts if we could visit the school we had toured a year earlier. I wanted to see if Iraqi children were actually enrolled there now and getting an education. Everything I saw around me seemed to dictate the answer they would give. It was just too dangerous. A year before, we had stopped and asked directions from the Iraqis who lived in the neighborhood. Now we could not go anywhere near them, even in an armed convoy.

Normally I was the last to speak in our meetings with American and Iraqi officials, but when we sat down with army general George William Casey Jr., commander of American forces in Iraq, Senator Biden asked me to lead off. I remember thinking that fatigue might have boosted my seniority that day; we were all beat after our many meetings in the Green Zone and outside Fallujah, and the daytime heat had tested our stamina. General Casey looked worn-out as well. I asked him the basic question in Sun-tzu's *The Art of War:* "Who is the enemy?" Given that we were seeing what appeared to be coordinated attacks over long distances, I wanted to know if the enemy had a chain of command.

To these simple questions the general gave a convoluted answer, which I reduced to this: *We face scores of seemingly disconnected enemies, but occasionally we see well-coordinated attacks on American forces and the Iraqi government. That suggests some sort of chain of command, but we have not been able to put our finger on it.*

After dinner that evening, hosted by Ambassador John Negroponte, I spoke privately with a number of embassy personnel, including a career State Department employee who was an Arabic-speaking expert on the Middle East. These people were veterans, posted to Baghdad for long periods. That was my usual method for gathering facts on these trips: I would pay attention and ask questions in the official briefings put on by the brass, but would also speak informally with as many junior officials as I could. They were less invested in my accepting the doctrine espoused from the top. Often, they had to be careful about what they revealed, and I took that into account.

A number of the dinner guests accompanied us to the tarmac where our Black Hawks were waiting. As we donned our gear, I turned to the career State Department employee I had enjoyed talking with at dinner. I got in one last question:

"How are we doing?" He made eye contact and answered without a word, an almost imperceptible shake of the head.

We were all a little dispirited as we prepared to fly out that night. The enormous challenges our forces had to shoulder weighed on us and contributed to a sense of fatigue. We rode the Black Hawk roller coaster back to Camp Freedom and boarded our C-130 for a flight to Kuwait. The plane had been loaded with outbound cargo, and a single flag-draped coffin. Nothing was said about the American in the coffin. We had no way of knowing if it was a man or a woman, someone's son or daughter or parent, from a big city or a farming town, a recent high school graduate or a middle-aged member of the National Guard. Without a face, name, age, gender, and branch of service, that fallen American who had died in the Cradle of Civilization represented, for me, all 2,200 who had perished at that point in the war.

Our pilot, an Air National Guardsman, said there was room for one of us to come forward and sit in the jump seat on the flight deck. There were no takers among my colleagues, so I said I would.

I sat next to the navigator, behind the pilot and copilot, and donned headphones so I could listen in as the crew ran down the checklist for our departure. Soon the four turboprop engines wound up and the heavy plane lumbered down the runway. When the pilot launched us into the sky, it was no gradual ascent; we went up fast in a corkscrew turn to minimize our chances of being swatted out of the air. Suddenly an alarm shrieked and the sky flashed just outside the cockpit windows. The pilot turned the plane onto its port wing and shouted, "Get the coordinates! Get the coordinates!" The engines, already at a high-pitched whine, suddenly made twice as much noise. The g-forces as we climbed out were greater than I had ever experienced. I waited for a bang, something hitting the plane. Soon the angle of ascent became less acute, the g-forces stopped pushing us into our seats, and my headphones were quiet as the pilots leveled off at higher altitude. The pilot throttled back and headed south toward Kuwait. We left the lights of Baghdad behind and settled into a long flight over a largely dark and empty Iraq. We flew in silence until the copilot said, "Anybody got a cigarette?" That broke the anxiety and everyone seemed to breathe again. Their manner, more than anything, made me think this was not a routine event.

Later, we saw points of yellow light burning in the darkness ahead. They were the oil wells of Kuwait burning off gas vapors. The crew talked a bit more about Baghdad and the emergency alarm. Had someone on the ground shot at us? They doubted it, but I wondered if they doubted it for my benefit; so I would play down the "get the coordinates" drama when the other senators and I compared notes later in Kuwait. The pilots told me the plane is equipped with automatic defenses against ground attack; the flashes we saw outside the cockpit were onboard flares the system had deployed to create multiple targets for any shoulder-fired missile streaking our way. The pilot said any number of things on the ground could have set off the C-130's defenses, even a flash of light from a mechanic striking an arc with a stick welder.

We spent the night in Kuwait and then flew to Bahrain to attend a conference on the Middle East. From there it was on to Jerusalem, where we arranged a last-minute meeting with

Israeli prime minister Ariel Sharon. He greeted us warmly, in his avuncular manner, and said, "Welcome to Jerusalem, now and forever the eternal capital of Israel."

When it was my turn to speak in our meeting, I told the prime minister that American public support for the war in Iraq was waning, and that change in opinion was likely to be reflected in our congressional elections. American lawmakers who were backing President Bush and "stay the course" in Iraq could be on the way out. Sharon might soon be dealing with American lawmakers who had run for office promising the voters a swift exit from Iraq. It was a prediction that would certainly come true in my own race in 2006. My Democratic challenger promised to bring the troops out within six months. I told the prime minister that a headlong rush for the door in Iraq, prompted by politics at home in the United States, would leave chaos behind, two hundred miles from the Israeli border. I thought our success in Iraq depended on a regional approach to peace, including progress on talks between Israelis and Palestinians.

I was not sure I had the prime minister's attention. He had barely listened to my senior colleagues. He was affording us the courtesy of an official meeting, but it was just that, a courtesy.

To be fair, we could not have chosen a more difficult time to call on the Israeli leader. The Knesset was in turmoil and he was preoccupied with his own political issues. In the brief time allotted us, he often looked over his shoulder to take papers from an aide, whisper a few words, and then read those papers while the senators tried to engage him in dialogue.

I felt very strongly about regional peace, especially since September 11, 2001. Our success in the Middle East depends on what our Founding Fathers must have believed when they designed the Great Seal of the United States, which appears on the back of the one-dollar bill and elsewhere: an eagle grasping arrows in one claw and an olive branch in the other. I had no success trying to get that point across to the Israeli prime minister, nor even to my own president.

In the fall of 2006, President Bush came to Capitol Hill to meet with the Republican caucus, again in the Mansfield Room, where the president had gone on that "private" rant reported by the well-sourced Howard Fineman of *Newsweek*. As we mingled over coffee and pastries and waited for the president to arrive, even the most jaded veteran senators sensed the added excitement of a presidential visit. It was not exactly the State of the Union address, but there was a definite buzz in the room. When the president was about to arrive Majority Leader Frist asked us to take our seats. The president made his entrance to the usual cheers and standing ovation. Hours later he would fly to Europe to enlist other nations in our efforts to prevent Iran from developing nuclear weapons. I was long past waiting for my fellow Republican senators to challenge the president on any of his policies. They had been absorbed into the institution, and dissent and valid questioning were rare. I did have a few thoughts of my own on his impending visit to Europe. When the president acknowledged me, I called his attention to the Seal of the President of the United States, modeled after the Founders' Great Seal of the United States. I talked about the two potent powers in the bald eagle's grasp, the arrows of war and the olive branch of peace. It was the same point that had gotten so many talk-radio listeners spitting mad at me in the days after September 11. I asked the president whether our success in the greater Middle East, including the Iranian nuclear weapons program, depended on how we waged both powers that the eagle commanded.

The president refused to address my question head-on. He paused for the briefest moment, called me, "Lincoln," and said it was interesting that the eagle's head is turned toward the claw that holds the olive branch. It was not that way in the beginning, he said. President Truman had ordered the seal redesigned at the end of World War II. Before Truman, our commanders in chief stood behind a seal that showed the eagle with its head turned toward the claw that grasps the arrows.

Truman, of course, is the only man in history ever to shoulder the awesome moral responsibility of destroying an enemy with nuclear weapons. The thirty-third president of the United States had vanquished Japan and ended the war, but had killed an enormous number of civilians in the process.

It made sense to me that Truman might not think war, or the threat of war, was the only way to meet future challenges. I was betting that from his lonely pinnacle in history he would see the wisdom of waging peace just as fiercely.

President Bush would not engage me on this. He dodged my point with a trivial anecdote, then looked around the room for another question. He would not utter a syllable to suggest that our chance of succeeding in the Middle East might depend on anything other than the arrows of war.

16

STANDING IN FOR THE PRESIDENT

In early 2006, I was looking ahead to the eleventh campaign of my career, and the first primary campaign of the lot. In heavily Democratic Rhode Island, Republicans go into a primary race with a certain amount of dread. A low turnout is inevitable and the outcome can hinge on a handful of votes. That makes the mechanics of a low-turnout primary radically different than those of a general election. Organizing the effort to identify and turn out your supporters is paramount.

I knew it was important in that September primary race to communicate early to the right-wing donor base and make Republicans realize they were not going to elect someone more conservative than the senator they already had. Rhode Island is a liberal Democratic state with a long tradition of rejecting conservatives. Grover Norquist, the right-wing activist who heads Americans for Tax Reform, saw the same scenario and urged Republicans to stay with me, no matter how angry they were with my voting record. As he told a reporter, "A Republican from Rhode Island is a gift from God."

I knew I would face a primary in 2006 because the wing of the party that wanted a rubber-stamp Congress, that demands absolute loyalty to President Bush on every vote, was out to punish me. The question was, How well financed would my challenger be? I heard rumors that the right-wing fund-raising juggernaut, the Club for Growth, was planning to bankroll the effort to unseat me.

I called the club's executive director, Patrick Toomey, a former Rhode Islander who had moved to Pennsylvania, been elected to Congress, and had nearly unseated Republican senator Arlen Specter in a 2004 primary. I wanted to talk about my primary race, but this was too important to do impersonally over the phone. I wanted to meet with Mr. Toomey privately, face-to-face. Every race is difficult for a Rhode Island Republican; first having to best an energetic and well-financed primary opponent makes the job infinitely more difficult. That is what I told Mr. Toomey when we sat down together. Given his Rhode Island roots, I did not have to remind him that out of thirty-eight state senators there were five Republicans, and out of seventy-five House members there were fifteen Republicans. Roughly 10 percent of registered voters in Rhode Island are Republican.

I told Mr. Toomey that if the Club for Growth brought its awesome fund-raising prowess to bear against me it could only end up electing a Democrat in November. It might even cost Republicans control of the Senate and, with that control, the chairmanship of every committee. The Democrats were already out there saying, *We have to beat Chafee. If we can't win Rhode Island, we can't win the Senate.*

Mr. Toomey acknowledged that the Club for Growth had a reputation for collecting scalps, unseating moderate Republicans in primary contests. Then, more often than not, they would lose the seat to a Democrat in the general election. He told me the club was getting out of that business and had learned to pick its fights more carefully; its new policy was to focus on races where the polls showed that the club's favorite Republican in the primary could go on to defeat the Democrat.

In the spring of 2006, every Rhode Island poll showed that I was the only Republican who stood a chance in November. I was polling ahead of my Democratic challenger at the time, which was remarkable given the difficult climate for Republicans in the Northeast. Voters here wanted to rebuke President Bush for his five years of damage done and discord sown. It would be difficult enough for an incumbent Republican to win the in-cycle Senate seat from Rhode Island, given the deep unpopularity of the Bush presidency. A newly minted Republican nominated with great enthusiasm by the far right would be utterly crushed in November. That was the lay of the land, obvious to even the most casual observers of Rhode Island politics.

As the campaign season neared and the juices started to flow, the Club for Growth talked itself out of its own sensible analysis and jumped into my primary race with both feet. It raised millions and buried my constituents in anti-Chafee ads. The simple truth was that my challenger was an extremist's extremist—a clashist of the first order—and that made him irresistible to the club's devotees of ideological purity. He might have been an appealing Republican candidate in a Deep South or Rocky Mountain precinct, but in the state of Rhode Island, he was utter folly.

My organization was in top form in that primary race. Campaign staffers worked hard to identify every constituency we needed to turn out. I did well in the debates. And, there were three unforeseen events that worked greatly in my favor, producing a record turnout for a Republican primary in Rhode Island.

One: There were no hotly contested primary races on the Democratic side, a rarity in Rhode Island; unaffiliated voters who had never before voted in a Republican primary were attracted to my race instead. My supporters told me, *I'm breaking out in hives voting in a Republican primary* and *I hope none of my friends see me standing in this line* and *My father's spinning in his grave that I'm voting Republican!*

Two: A new state law ordered the schools closed on primary day, and having the children at home served as a reminder to parents, *Today is primary day, I should go vote.*

Three: The weather was on my side. My opponent's supporters would have kayaked and snorkeled through a hurricane storm surge to knock me out of office. Instead, we had a gorgeous fall day that was all to my benefit. As I traveled the state on primary day, I was elated to see people flocking to the polls.

My opponent, meanwhile, was certain of victory until the final hours, adamantly so. When his sound defeat became apparent on election night, he was unable to speak with reporters.

I would live to fight in November, but the club had damaged me. I had spent millions countering its negative ads. Now, with resources drained, I faced the Democratic candidate in a heavily Democratic state. A former Rhode Island attorney general and United States attorney, Sheldon Whitehouse had breezed through a noncompetitive primary and was sitting on enormous cash reserves raised by a Democratic apparatus that sensed victory in the race for Senate control.

Buoyed by polls that showed Republicans weighed down by the president and a rubber-stamp Congress, Democratic donors poured money into key Senate races around the country, including mine. They firehosed me with criticism, linking me to the right-wing failures of the president and the Senate. I was well known for fighting the president and the GOP leadership, and, indeed, had gone through a costly primary challenge because of it. My opponent, on the other hand, had a record of ducking fights, which I relished to highlight. As U.S. attorney he had declined to prosecute Buddy Cianci, the famously corrupt but popular mayor of Providence. Meg Curran, his successor as U.S. attorney, rolled up the case and sent Cianci to federal prison. My Democratic opponent had also passed on prosecuting fraud by the politically connected at Roger Williams Hospital, another case where justice was served after his departure.

I was the only candidate in the race with a record of standing up to entrenched powers, but a parade of Democratic Bush enablers came to Rhode Island to campaign for my opponent. I was both irked and amused at this irony of politics. Senators Harry Reid, Chuck Schumer, Hillary Clinton, and others who had voted for the war in Iraq, urged my constituents, at this critical time in history, to elect one more of their own, as I saw it.

In any event, Mr. Whitehouse ran not against me, but against President Bush, whose approval rating in Rhode Island was abysmal. Even with the incumbency on my side—that important home field advantage—I found it difficult to raise the money I needed to focus the race. It was far easier to raise money in 2000 when I was a Senate newcomer. The Rockefeller Republicans who favored women's rights, fiscal responsibility, and a sensible stand on the environment, and who did not see the hot-button social issues as national priorities, had stopped giving to Republicans. Will they ever come back to the party? Not in any future that I can foresee. Republicans are seen now as obstinate, unable to adapt, obsessed with contentious social issues. That damaged reputation is likely to persist for a long time.

The campaign approach that humbled Republicans in 2006 was no accident or unlucky circumstance; it was by design and policy. The leadership wanted us focused on abortion, gay marriage, and the flag. I believe the voters would have been better served by a debate on the deteriorating situation in the Middle East, on millions more losing their health insurance, and on why the poor were becoming poorer as the rich became superrich.

The leadership unfolded the strategy in June and July of 2006, before our traditional August recess. Because we controlled the agenda, we made the Senate spend the entire summer debating the three emotional and divisive issues.

The Republican-sponsored bill on abortion would make it

a felony for an adult to assist a minor in crossing state lines to evade local restrictions on abortion. Republicans wanted gay marriage in the national political dialogue that fall, too, but there was a problem: The fifty states owned the issue. How could we in Congress claim jurisdiction? The leadership came up with the radical idea of transforming a legislative state issue into a constitutional federal issue. We would propose a constitutional amendment on gay marriage, one that would ban states from enacting their own social compacts on the issue.

Republicans are generally seen as the party that favors independence at the state level, allowing the fifty state legislatures to function as legislative laboratories to see how different solutions to problems work in the real world. But now we wanted to amend the U.S. Constitution to forbid any state to allow gays to marry. Congress itself would not ban gay marriage; but the amendment would prevent liberal states from recognizing gay couples as married, even if most citizens in that state wanted such a law enacted. Democracy might be everything in Iraq, but we were declaring an urgent need to rein it in here at home.

Republicans also wanted to open up our sacred Constitution to an amendment on flag burning, or flag desecration as it was called. It would get us arguing endlessly about what was desecration and what was free speech, a nightmare for most, but the sweetest of dreams for Republican strategists. It would whip up the emotions of the base and get those voters to the polls.

In my opinion, some members of Congress desecrated the flag every day by wearing flag pins on their lapels while voting to divide Americans and restrict freedom. But that was their right, their freedom of speech; I hardly wanted to amend the Constitution over it.

In any event, this Republican-sponsored amendment to the Constitution would create a restriction on the First Amendment. It would authorize Congress to pass laws fining or jailing anyone who desecrated the flag.

It was a philosophically incoherent platform that we debated that summer. We were both for and against state's rights: If a state wanted to restrict abortion, that was good; if a state wanted to allow gays to marry, that was bad, and we would amend the U.S. Constitution to prevent it.

The abortion law and the gay marriage amendment were both defeated before the 2006 election; the abortion law was defeated narrowly, the gay marriage amendment overwhelmingly. Win or lose, the political effect was the same; Republicans could get out there on the campaign trail and attack Democrats who had voted against the GOP position on these issues.

Everyone knew the flag desecration vote would be close. Veterans groups, the American Legion in particular, were energized on the issue and were after me to vote in favor. Here I was in the middle of a primary campaign and veterans were telling me they needed my vote to make the difference. Everyone knew the margin was razor thin. *If you vote yea, we win,* the veterans said. And they reminded me: *We vote in Republican primaries.*

In meetings with veterans I argued that almost no one desecrates the flag. To the contrary, September 11 had inspired millions of Americans to start flying the flag for the first time in their lives. Republicans were whipping up veterans over a nonissue for short-term political gain in November.

I had not seen an American protester burn an American flag in thirty years. It was just plain wrong and irresponsible to use our own partisan political agenda to poison fifty statehouses with these emotional nonissues. We would be sabotaging the real work our state lawmakers had to accomplish—improving schools, roads, and bridges, providing public safety—just as we had sabotaged our own work in Washington.

The House passed the amendment by the required two-thirds majority and President Bush was delighted to announce that he would sign the legislation if the Senate followed suit. It would take a two-thirds majority there as well, sixty-seven senators, to send the flag-desecration amendment to the states, the support of three-quarters of whom would be needed for ratification.

After a dramatic call of the roll on a proposal to amend our Constitution, it failed by one vote. I had never been prouder to cast a vote, a vote to uphold the First Amendment. Only three Republicans were so minded. I found myself allied with senators Bob Bennett of Utah and Mitch McConnell of Kentucky. We were on opposite sides on many issues, but we stood together to block this effort to divide America and abridge our constitutional right of free speech.

What a disgrace. Only thirty-one Democrats and three Republicans thought the Constitution should be off limits to election-year tampering. While parroting President Bush's rhetoric about terrorists who "hate our freedoms," sixty-six United States senators thought it was right to restrict free political speech in America. That, or they rolled their eyes and voted yea purely to duck a fight.

I found many of the yea votes baffling. Using the flag for

political gain was the real desecration; and, in the end, there was no political gain for Republicans. Most Americans now recognized that we had played to their fears and emotions in 2002 and 2004. The hoopla over flag desecration was just one more misguided scheme, and it backfired on us in 2006. The Republican hat trick on the flag, abortion, and gays was never there to be exploited, but our leaders refused to see that.

When the dust settled in November 2006, my career in the United States Senate was over. Of the seven hotly contested Senate seats, Democrats had won the six they needed to gain control. Voters had rejected extremism, as they had done in 2000, before September 11. The fear-filled post–September 11 world that Republicans thought would go on forever had come to an end. This time, it was not just the hard-liners who fell; I was the moderate-to-liberal Republican casualty.

My party had tried to hold power by stoking the fear of terrorism and dividing America on the wedge issues, but that moment in history had passed. Voters were thinking with their brains again, not their adrenal glands. They no longer jumped at the orange and red terror alerts the administration sounded at will. Out went Conrad Burns in Montana, Mike DeWine in Ohio, Rick Santorum in Pennsylvania, Jim Talent in Missouri, George Allen in Virginia, and me. Incumbents are hard to beat; it means something important when so many lose.

We were still bruised when we returned to Washington to wrap up the 109th Congress and elect new leadership for the 110th. But would it really be new? The thoughtful senator Lamar Alexander wanted to be the Republican whip, our second-highest leadership position, and he worked hard to promote his candidacy, and to win. He initially had the votes to join the leadership, and I thought he would reflect well on our party and show that we were ready to acknowledge the voters' message and chart a new course. Former majority leader Trent Lott made a late challenge for minority whip and prevailed over Senator Alexander by one vote. Two senators pledged to Senator Alexander switched in the secret balloting.

Back in 2000 the voters told us we were too extreme and divisive. The party responded by shunning a leadership bid by Senator Pete Domenici of New Mexico, as it now shunned Senator Alexander. Neither Republican senator is a liberal by any stretch, but at least they were not known for defaulting to right-wing groupthink on every issue. The voters repeated their 2000 message to us in 2006. As a party, our answer was: *We're not changing. We don't hear you.*

The president was not listening to the voters, either. They had repudiated his war, and he responded by sending more troops. *I'm surging. And no one can stop me.*

He was as defiant in failure as the new Republican minority in Congress.

17

STRONG NEIGHBORS

In the 2000 campaign, Governor Bush courted the Hispanic vote by pledging to focus constructively on Latin America, to put that important region at the very center of his agenda on foreign affairs. He touted his record in Texas, a border state with a large Hispanic population. His handsome and well-spoken nephew, George P. Bush, became a star of the 2000 Republican Convention when he addressed the delegates in Spanish.

That summer, George W. Bush said Latin American had been a mere "afterthought" to the Clinton administration. "Those who ignore Latin America do not fully understand America itself. And those who ignore our hemisphere do not fully understand American interests."

The future president's "chief foreign policy adviser," Condoleezza Rice, said his guiding philosophy would be, "You start with strong neighbors and reach out from there."

When President Bush took the oath of office the following

January, I was eager to work with him on his vision for Latin America, given my chairmanship of the Foreign Relations Subcommittee on the Western Hemisphere. It was my job to understand and track issues affecting our relations with every country between Hudson Bay and Cape Horn. I already knew Canada reasonably well, having lived there for seven years when I was shoeing horses on the race circuit. I was eager now to learn more about the countries to our south. It was almost never easy to get away and travel the region; I had a young family and many other commitments, but I took my responsibilities as chairman seriously and thought it was important to meet our neighbors, and to listen and learn. I traveled through Latin America with leaders of every political stripe, from President Clinton to Senator Jesse Helms. I especially enjoyed traveling with Senator Chris Dodd of Connecticut, the ranking Democrat on the subcommittee. He speaks Spanish fluently, and I appreciated his high energy and good humor.

What I saw in Latin America at the beginning of my tenure was encouraging. When you see positive change happening you want to be a part of it and help to build on it. Despite the "strong neighbors" rhetoric, the Bush-Cheney team had another view. In 2002, President Bush nominated the polarizing Otto Reich as assistant secretary of state for western hemisphere affairs. Reich was a minor figure implicated in the Iran-Contra scandal in the 1980s; government investigators said he had illegally used tax dollars to spread pro-Contra propaganda inside the United States. When it became clear the Senate would not confirm Reich in this new post, the president resorted to the tactic he had used to seat John Bolton at the United Nations: He waited until the Senate left town, then installed his unconfirmable nominee with a recess appointment. The president had returned to form, showing contempt for both Congress and the Latin American governments that took a dim view of Reich and his extreme politics.

After launching the war in Iraq in 2003, the president paid little notice to Latin America. This neglect of our own hemisphere, sadly, may be a blessing in disguise, given the record of the Bush-Cheney administration in foreign affairs; but our next president, with all urgency, must reengage our neighbors.

Phenomenal change occurred in Latin America in the 1990s, and accelerated after the White House turned its attention to the shapeless and ill-defined war on terror. There has been "a revolution of participation," a phrase attributed to the controversial president of Venezuela, Hugo Chávez. New leaders have come up from farms and villages; wealthy landowners are no longer entitled to rule by the happenstance of birth alone. Aside from Cuba, every country south of our border has evolved into a democracy on its own, with an elected head of state who is restrained, to a greater or lesser degree, by an elected legislature. New leaders emphasized their desire to improve the lives of their poorest citizens. Among the new generation are Luiz Inácio Lula da Silva in Brazil, Evo Morales in Bolivia, Rafael Correa in Ecuador. Almost every one of our southern neighbors had an emerging middle class and the economic growth that results when ordinary people have buying power. That is why we see an unmistakable Chinese presence in many important capitals to our south. In my tenure, it was not unusual to arrive for a meeting with government officials in Buenos Aires, Caracas, or Santiago and find a delegation from the People's Republic of China just leaving, or waiting to go in after we left. The Chinese recognize Latin America as a modernizing continent with enormous economic potential; they are active in the region, striking deals on timber, crops, minerals, oil, and natural gas. Taking the long view, the Chinese are making friends and amassing influence in our own backyard.

In 2000, in Mexico City, I was privileged to witness the peaceful transfer of power in what had been a one-party political system for seventy years, controlled by PRI, the Institutional Revolutionary Party. President Ernesto Zedillo removed the ceremonial sash he wore and placed it over the shoulder of his newly elected successor. There was no coup, no riots, no chaos; change was in the air, and when the time was right, it happened. President Vicente Fox beamed as he accepted the sash, a symbol of the power he had received by the will of the Mexican people.

In January 2001, I went to Cuba with Senator Arlen Specter. The land has a unique topography; flat, green, and fertile in the west, stretching east into the towering Sierra Maestra, where Castro and his guerrillas operated in the revolution. I was struck by how the 745-mile-long island seems lost in time. Everything I saw there was modest and humble, but not what I could call poverty-stricken. No one appeared hungry, homeless, or sick; indeed, the island has far better health care and education than many of its wealthier neighbors. But it was a strange experience to get off a modern jet at José Martí International Airport and then share the road with horse-drawn carts on the drive into Havana. Many motorists drove fifty-year-old Soviet and American cars that ran on parts fabricated in backyard machine shops. Most buildings look as if they have not been painted since 1959, when Castro overthrew the dictatorship of Fulgencio Batista and set up his own.

At night, the busiest streets in Havana are dark or dimly lit by a flickering streetlight or two. It is so unlike other capitals, where commercial districts shine bright with the effects of globalization, the neon signs that advertise the American consumer franchises spreading rapidly around the world. There is nothing like that in Havana.

In this totalitarian state, we were permitted to meet with leading dissidents working under the Varela Project, a movement to advance democratic political reform. They seemed a serious organization, but I wondered: Were they professional dissidents? Did the Communist government permit them to exist only as a public relations gesture to foreign critics?

At a state dinner, our gray-bearded host in his trademark military fatigues touted his country's low infant mortality, its high number of doctors per capita, and the literacy of the Cuban people. My snap impression of Fidel Castro was that he is smart, quick with a laugh, and has charisma. At the same time, I am well aware of his ruthless history. Senator Specter meant to say something provocative at dinner. He asked the president, "When are you going to have free elections here in Cuba?" Castro shot back, "You mean like in Florida?"

In the course of a boisterous dinner that went on for hours—ending at 3:00 A.M.—I asked the Cuban president, mischievously, whether he supported calls for an end to the U.S. embargo. Even conservative senators from farm states were working to normalize trade with Cuba in the interest of opening new markets for their crops. Votes to end the embargo were increasingly close. Was it a given that Castro supported these efforts? I was betting he did not. Ending the embargo imposed in 1962 would change the way he had done business for almost his entire reign. He knew what I was getting at: The embargo works for him in a perverse way. Having a reason to lash out at the United States has been his meal ticket with the Cuban people for a long time.

He dodged my question and zoomed off on a tangent that I no longer recall. But I was satisfied; by not answering my question, he had answered it.

It was clear to me that day in Havana that the rest of the world is far ahead of us in planning for the end of the octogenarian president's rule. Nations in Europe, Asia, and Latin America were positioning themselves to take advantage of trade in the next Cuba. There was slight evidence of a robust foreign invasion at the time, but it was starting.

In 2001, in Peru, I saw something that reminded me of President Clinton's visit to Cartagena the year before. Senator Specter and I met with Peruvian president Alejandro Toledo, who was born in modest circumstances and rose to become Peru's first president of indigenous ancestry. The day after we arrived, President Toledo planned to fly in to a village high in the Andes to announce some improvement to the health care or education of its residents. Senator Specter declined an invitation to accompany President Toledo; he had already arranged a long day of meetings with American business groups. Having sat through many long meetings on these visits south, I told Senator Specter I would give his regards to the Andean villagers. President Toledo's official plane carried us up into the mountain city of Cuzco, where we boarded a helicopter for the final leg of the flight into even-higher altitudes. The air was so thin that a few of the foreigners traveling with President Toledo had to go on oxygen. They were Israeli physicians and surgeons who had volunteered to treat scores of Peruvian workers injured and burned in a recent factory explosion. The doctors had worked around the clock for days, and, perhaps because of their fatigue, the lack of oxygen hit them hard. I felt some ill effects myself and walked a little slower than usual to avoid getting winded in the mountain air. I stayed in the background as President Toledo stepped up to speak from a makeshift platform, using a microphone wired to a car battery. A moment later, he identified me to the crowd of about a hundred villagers. If he said my name, I missed it, but I was able to understand the meaning of the Spanish words *senador* and *Estados Unidos*. When the villagers applauded, I thought of Cartagena, back when "an age of lasting peace beckoned." This spontaneous applause from the Peruvians was not for me, of course; it was for the country I represented. I suspect it would not happen again if I returned to that same village today. With better leadership, we can get that friendship back, the warm association that foreign nations had for America at the end of the cold war. And we have to get it back. That has to become our goal when power changes hands in January 2009.

In 2002, in Chile, I met with President Ricardo Lagos in the same palace where President Salvador Allende met his end in the military coup of 1973, by assassination or suicide, depending on which story you believe. Nearly thirty years later, a center-left president had been elected to lead a nation so recently ruled by a cruel tyrant, General Augusto Pinochet.

Chileans were looking ahead; they were not focused on retribution. They had put the Pinochet nightmare behind them and had largely healed as a people. It was that focus on the future, coupled with a healthy dose of free market enterprise, that enabled them to build their country into a leading model of prosperity in Latin America. They had a stable government, fair opposition, and a good political dynamic under way.

Argentina, in contrast, had a financial meltdown in 2002. People rioted in the streets just before we arrived. Television news had overplayed the unrest—I saw only a few stores with windows smashed—but the financial problems in Argentina were very real. I wanted to understand how the Senate could help, perhaps by supporting efforts to restructure the country's debt, or some other form of relief that might help set the Argentines on the same path to peace and prosperity as their Chilean neighbors.

When we crossed the wide Río de la Plata, into neighboring Uruguay, I met with President Jorge Batlle, who insisted that our decades-old battle against the narcotics trade was not working. He praised our efforts but urged us to consider legalizing drugs instead. The enormous profits in illegal drugs had an insidious effect on all levels of the economy, including the banking system, he said. Illicit drug money had corrupted some officials in law enforcement, the courts, and the legislatures. President Batlle advocated the Libertarian approach: legalize drugs to reduce their street value and put the cartels out of business, then regulate and tax those drugs as we do tobacco and alcohol. I doubt that our culture would allow that. Most Americans do not want heroin and crack cocaine sold on store shelves as if they were no more addictive or dangerous than cigarettes and alcohol. I might have expected a young firebrand to advocate that radical break with the crime-and-punishment model, but President Batlle was seventy-four when I met him.

We will probably have this debate in the United States, but not because Latin America is having it. The debate will come when we can no longer avoid confronting the destabilizing heroin trade in Afghanistan, nine thousand miles east of where I sat with President Batlle. We freed Afghanistan at a cost of billions and, more importantly, the lives of many American and NATO troops. Liberated from Taliban rule, Afghan poppy growers are organizing gangs of private gun-men to guard their lucrative crops. At some point we will have to acknowledge that our new democratic ally in the war on terror is on the opposite side in our war on drugs.

On a trip to Colombia, I spoke to American crop-duster pilots working on the eradication component of our three-pronged antidrug campaign: eradication, interdiction, substitution. We landed in the jungle, on what seemed a dangerous little airstrip in Tres Esquinas, a town in the Putumayo region. After getting the official briefings, I went outside to speak privately with the crop dusters. One pilot, a young father with children back home in Illinois, had come south to work on coca eradication. He thought the antidrug campaign was working, but I kept in mind that he was drawing terrific money from the American taxpayer, a lot more than he could make spraying for bugs and worms in the soybean and corn-fields of Illinois. But no one was likely to shoot at him back home; here, he told me, he sits on a piece of plate steel when he flies. Many coca growers carry rifles and would rather that American pilots not spray herbicides on their crops.

Early in my tenure I had voted for Plan Colombia, as it was called, a $1 billion aid package that included major efforts to suppress the cocaine trade. I was quickly criticized by peace groups who accused me of encouraging more bloodshed in the struggle between the Marxist FARC and private paramilitary forces hired by ranchers and other large landowners. Those were the forces contributing to the lawlessness of Colombia, the heavily armed FARC and the equally brutal and heavily funded "paras." They are called left and right in the newspapers, but they are fighting over narcotics first, not politics.

I saw other private armies and lawless men operating on the continent, notably in the so-called Tri-Border Region, a kind of Wild West where the frontiers of Argentina, Brazil, and Paraguay meet. Criminals and smugglers of every stripe move through the region, dealing in weapons, currency, and drugs. On a bridge over the Paraná River, we saw pedestrians and truck drivers openly trading contraband across the border. There was something resembling a customs check, but it was overwhelmed. We heard talk of foreigners with al-Qaeda sympathies operating in the lawless region, but proof was elusive.

My first trip to Venezuela was with Congressman Cass Ballenger, a Republican from a conservative district in the foothills of North Carolina. He had formed an unlikely friendship with President Hugo Chávez, an ex-paratrooper who had been imprisoned in 1992, after leading an unsuccessful military coup, then went on to win the Venezuelan presidency six years later at the ballot box. The Democratic Action and Social Christian parties had dominated Venezuelan politics for forty years; Chavez mounted a third-party challenge and won 56 percent of the popular vote. Such was their friendship that Congressman Ballenger, age seventy-four, hosted President Chávez at a backyard barbecue in Hickory, North Carolina, in the spring of 2001. It was in the spirit of the Ping-Pong Diplomacy of the Nixon era that did so much to improve relations between the United States and China. The cookout in Ballenger's backyard came much to the astonishment of his neighbors, whom he invited over the fence to meet the burly Venezuelan so often caricatured as a "foreign dictator."

"His rhetoric is worse than his actions," Congressman Ballenger once said of the man whose country was the fourth leading supplier of oil to the United States. I liked the fact that a conservative Republican lawmaker and the head of the United Socialist Party of Venezuela had found a way to talk together, eat together, and accentuate what they had in common. Once acquainted, they found they had little desire to demonize each other.

Three years later, in 2006, Chávez literally demonized President Bush in a world-televised address at U.N. headquarters in New York. Our president had addressed the General Assembly a day earlier. To laughter from the world community, an animated Chávez made the sign of the cross and said, "Yesterday, the Devil came here. Right here. Right here. And it smells of sulfur still today, this table that I am now standing in front of. Yesterday, ladies of gentlemen, from this rostrum, the president of the United States, the gentleman to whom I refer as 'the Devil,' came here, talking as if he owned the world. Truly, as the owner of the world. . . ."

Representative Ballenger and I met with Chávez in Miraflores, the presidential palace in Caracas, on April 26, 2002. That was just two weeks after some factions in the Venezuelan military had attempted to unseat, and, perhaps murder him and install Pedro Carmona, a right-wing businessman who fled to Miami after ruling Venezuela for a day and a half. In his thirty-six hours in power, Carmona disbanded the National Assembly and the Supreme Court, suspended the Constitution, and revoked forty-nine laws that had formed the basis of Chávez's popularity with the poor. Armed men seen protecting Carmona were identified as bodyguards in the employ of a powerful family in the petrochemical industry. The head of the Venezuelan state airline said "a highly conservative sector of the business community" was out to seize power through Carmona.

When Venezuelans saw business and social elites dismantling their liberties, they poured into the streets to demand their president's freedom. The conspiracy, by then, was unraveling on its own as the men behind it double- and triple-crossed one another in attempts to grab power for themselves. Chávez supporters disabled the army's helicopter gunships and the presidential jetliner to prevent their being used to spirit the captive president out of the country. Commandos loyal to Chávez found him imprisoned on Orchila, an island in the Caribbean. They arrested his captors and brought him back to the Miraflores Palace.

Two weeks later, as Chávez recounted the events of the coup for us, I was surprised he was not angry. His tone was conciliatory, and introspective. He had almost become another Allende, but I heard no vow of retribution. It was remarkable. He said he would talk more with his powerful critics in industry, organized labor, and the media. *We cannot have people marching on Miraflores and firing guns and being killed.*

In the course of conversation, President Chávez allowed as how, unlike some of his neighboring heads of state, he had never been afforded an Oval Office photo opportunity.

In subsequent years, I sometimes wondered if this blow to the Venezuelan leader's ego had played a part in escalating his fiery rhetoric, and his displays of seeking friendship among America's adversaries, in Cuba, Iran, and elsewhere. I never got the sense that Chávez enjoys being our enemy. Fidel Castro has made a living off playing David to the United States' Goliath, but Castro is the past. Chávez is up-and-coming. It would make sense for him to forge the best possible relationship with us, and us with him. Of course, the clashists who came to power with President Bush would have none of that; they need every nation labeled and driven into one of two camps: all good or all bad.

When the clashists fanned the flames of enmity with Chávez, he ran with it, applying his talent for anti-American oratory in extravagant ways. But I doubt that he ran for office in 1998 with that kind of presidency in mind.

After the attempted coup, Chávez raised taxes on American companies operating in Venezuela, then invited the Chinese to explore for new reserves in the rich Orinoco oil belt. In January 2007, Venezuelan lawmakers unanimously empowered him to rule by decree for eighteen months, and, in that time, to nationalize the oil and telecommunications industries. Reaction at the State Department followed the script: Deputy Secretary John Negroponte said Chávez "has been trying to export his kind of radical populism and I think his behavior is threatening to democracies in the region."

On January 18, 2005, Condoleezza Rice came before the Senate Foreign Relations Committee for confirmation as secretary of state. I asked her to speak to the verbal warfare going on between the White House and Chávez. How did it serve American interests?

Ms. Rice would not acknowledge that the Venezuelans had voted their president into office in free and fair elections. "It seems to me, to say derogatory things about him may be disrespectful to him, but also to the Venezuelan people," I said.

Ms. Rice said, "Well, I have nothing but good things to say about the Venezuelan people. They are a remarkable people. And if you notice, Senator Chafee, I was not making derogatory comments, I was simply recognizing that there are unhelpful and unconstructive trends going on in Venezuelan policies. This is not personal."

"And there aren't in Tajikistan? Uzbekistan? And Russia? Pakistan?" I said, naming countries she had praised, our so-called allies in the Bush-Cheney war on terror.

I wanted to pin her down on the issue of consistency; we were sending Americans to die for an unlikely Islamic democracy in Iraq while carrying on a cold war with a legitimately elected leader close to home.

Ms. Rice was at her immovable best, until I said, in exasperation, "Is it possible for you to say *something* positive about the Chávez administration?"

"It's pretty hard, Senator, to find something positive," she said. Viewed through the official White House lens, the freely elected government of Venezuela was all bad. I wanted the nominee to say one positive thing about a neighboring democracy. I never asked her to embrace that democracy or pretend we had no differences, just to step out of attack mode for a moment.

She could think of nothing positive, and my time was up. I told her, in closing, that this insistence on "magnifying our differences to some countries and magnifying our similarities to others" did not serve America. "I think trust is built with consistency," I said. "I don't see consistency."

The tragedy of this first decade of the new American century is that our leaders in the White House and in Congress were lost when it came to charting our way in a new era. With the cold war won and behind us, the clashists could make no sense of the world unless they organized it around a new global fight to last for generations, an enemy called "terror." And with Castro and Cuba hardly a threat anymore, they needed a Chávez and a Venezuela.

When I visited President Chávez in the Miraflores Palace in 2002, and again in 2005, I understood what Congressman Ballenger saw in him standing around the backyard barbeque in Hickory, North Carolina. Chávez is a big man with a big handshake and an irascible persona. I also met with his vice president, José Vicente Rangel, who struck me as less aggressive; he had very practical views on how to manage his country's enormous oil and gas wealth and mend relations with the United States.

In 2005, Chávez refused to meet with our delegation when he heard that Democratic senator Bill Nelson of Florida was with us. The senator had recently told reporters that President Bush was not being "tough enough" with the

Venezuelan president. The remark was probably intended for home consumption by anti-Castro Cuban Americans in Miami, but it was not lost on Chávez; he followed the American papers. He announced that he would meet with the American delegation as long as Senator Nelson was not included. We stuck together and encouraged the president to meet with all of us, without conditions. Finally, he agreed. My recollection is that he and Senator Nelson spoke privately for a few moments first, to clear the air.

That day, Chávez said something that stayed with me, probably because it was a sad commentary. He mentioned it very late in the meeting, as an aside, and frowned as he told it. That morning at breakfast, he said, his daughter asked him what he was planning to do all day. He ticked off the list of events and duties on his calendar, ending with . . . *and then I'm going to meet with some Americans.*

He told us that his seven-year-old responded: *Be careful.*

18

THE DUAL VICTORIES

Like every American, I looked at the facts and reached my own conclusion on whether President Bush and Vice President Cheney knew, before they ordered our troops into Iraq, that Saddam had no weapons of mass destruction. Behind the scenes, I think, key figures in the administration had a variety of reasons for wanting to topple the dictator. Some wanted the "total victory" that President George H. W. Bush wisely did not insist upon in the Gulf War in 1991. Some believed in spreading democracy by force. And some just could not stand the thought of Saddam controlling such vast oil reserves. But none were willing to suggest to the American people that their sons and daughters should fight and die for any of these reasons. Instead, the White House marketed the war on chemical, biological, and nuclear weapons and the threat of *"the smoking gun that could come in the form of a mushroom cloud."*

To me, the skit the president performed at a March 2004

dinner in Washington, in which he pretended to search for weapons of mass destruction under and behind the White House furniture—*"Nope, no weapons over there!"*—was a cynical admission that the reason he gave for the war had been a sham. It was obscene for him to joke about a falsehood that American troops had gone to their graves believing.

The president's duplicity on weapons of mass destruction may have colored my views on another important issue: whether he was acting in good faith when he pledged to work toward peace between Israel and the Palestinians. The key to success, he declared, would be the creation of a Palestinian state. This was groundbreaking. No American president had ever backed an independent Palestinian state. If President Bush meant to pursue a bold new peace plan in the region, I stood ready to help him succeed. I was in a position to do just that in January 2003, when I attained the chairmanship of the Committee on Foreign Relations' Near Eastern and South Asian Affairs Subcommittee. It was our job to provide oversight on foreign initiatives from Morocco to the Indian subcontinent, especially those affecting Israel, Jordan, Syria, Lebanon, and Egypt.

The president unveiled his Israeli-Arab peace plan on June 24, 2002, in a speech delivered in the Rose Garden. He pledged that America, for the first time, would support founding a Palestinian state in the West Bank and the Gaza Strip, the "disputed territories" that Israel had occupied since the end of the Six-Day War in 1967.

But that new Palestinian nation was not to be. As in Iraq, the president would make matters worse in the West Bank and Gaza, not better. Over the next five years, his actions on the peace process—importantly, his very *inaction*—seemed designed to ensure that the Palestinians would not achieve a homeland in the occupied territories.

Some may be credulous enough to believe the president sincerely worked for peace between Israel and the Palestinians; but, at this writing, the only people rejoicing in his policy are the leaders of Hamas, the terrorist group that triumphed in free Palestinian elections in 2006, and a minority of Israeli clashists who intend to fight their nation's every effort at peace with the Palestinians.

In early 2003, I was after the White House to articulate what it was trying to accomplish in the region. At that time, the best key we had for trying to understand the president's motives was an appearance by Deputy Secretary of Defense Paul Wolfowitz before the Senate Committee on Foreign Relations.

Mr. Wolfowitz, the administration figure most identified with the doctrine of regime change in Iraq, is often portrayed as one of the villains of the Bush-Cheney era. I am more charitable. Mr. Wolfowitz surprised the Senate now and again by deviating from the script and the politics of the moment. To be sure, there were times when he closely adhered to the talking points, and he and I had some memorable disputes on those occasions. But on May 22, 2003, he was the only administration figure willing to think expansively about how one American action in the Middle East might affect the outcome of another. I respected Paul Wolfowitz for that, and still do.

News reports from Iraq in May 2003 had Washington in a state of euphoria. We did indeed appear to be welcomed as liberators, as Vice President Cheney had predicted. Jubilant

Iraqis had danced in the streets as American soldiers pulled down the statue of the deposed dictator. The president, outfitted as a combat pilot, had made his triumphant landing on the carrier USS *Abraham Lincoln*. I believe this air of exhilaration might explain why Mr. Wolfowitz was so eager to paint the big picture on the broad canvas I offered him.

He told the Senate Committee on Foreign Relations that the Iraq war would help us do three things: spread democracy throughout the Arab world; make peace between Israel and the Palestinians; and withdraw American troops from around the Muslim holy sites of Mecca and Medina, in Saudi Arabia, thereby denying propaganda points to Osama bin Laden.

I offer that testimony here in its entirety because it is important to understanding how the president led us to dual failures in Iraq and on the Israeli peace process instead of the "dual victories" his deputy secretary of defense foresaw in 2003. Mr. Wolfowitz candidly told the Senate what the administration was thinking in the intoxicating days of "Mission Accomplished"—or what he thought it was thinking. The italics that follow are mine.

CHAFEE: It seems to me that we have thrown a rock into the pool that is the Middle East, and just for the sake of my question, if all goes well with restoring order in Iraq, what is the strategic vision of the ripples that are now going out from this rock? What is the strategic vision in the Middle East now?

WOLFOWITZ: I would say several things. I think some of them hopefully will happen even perhaps before some of the other results are achieved inside Iraq. I think one of the ripples is *a positive impact on the Arab-Israeli peace process,* and clearly we need it. We need to move that process forward. I think we have credibility, enormous credibility, not that we did not have it before. We have it more than we did before.

I think the removal of Saddam Hussein as somebody who was providing $25,000 to every terrorist family is already a sign that that is having a positive impact. I think a less direct, but maybe even more important impact is that I think the defeat of Saddam Hussein has improved the strategic position of Saudi Arabia, and the events of the terrorist attack of ten days ago demonstrate that they need an improved strategic position.

What do I mean by an improved strategic position? I mean, one, *that the Saudis do not have to worry about a hostile regime to their north that was actively interested in undermining them,* but secondly, and maybe even more important, because of the successful operation in Iraq, Secretary Rumsfeld and his Saudi counterpart two or three weeks ago now were able to agree that most U.S. forces could come out of Saudi Arabia.

That gives the Government of Saudi Arabia some freedom it has not had for 12 years *to not be constantly subject to the charge leveled by Osama bin Laden that they are basing so-called Crusader forces on Arab territory,* and hopefully that also rebounds back into the peace process, because I think one of the things that was missing in the Camp David and Taba negotiations in 2000 and early 2001 was that the Saudis and the Egyptians did not step up to the plate, so those are big effects.

But finally, I think if we could *get to the point where Iraq can be a model of free representative democratic government by an Arab standard,* not—I mean, Japan's democracy is different from ours, is different from England's. Iraq's democracy will be different from Poland's and different from Romania's. But if Iraq can present an example to the Arab world that is a positive example, I think, just as we have seen the power of example operate in East Asia or in Europe, I think it can operate in the Middle East in the Muslim world.

It is hard to say exactly how. It is not a domino effect. It is not that Iraq affects the country next door, which affects—it is not a physical thing. It is a psychological and political and sort of moral impact, which can be large.

I just met with the foreign minister of Morocco, who was very emphatic about what a positive effect the demise of the Saddam Hussein regime had on the Arab world, and Morocco is one of those countries that is making some of the most courageous steps to try to expand the realm of political freedom and democracy in that country.

CHAFEE: Could you elaborate, please, on how you see this affecting progress between the Palestinians and the Israelis?

WOLFOWITZ: Well, as I said, it removes a factor that was deeply opposed to progress. In fact, it is not at all insignificant that when the Arab League organized against Anwar Sadat's peace efforts 20 year ago, it was led by Saddam Hussein and it was known as the Baghdad Summit. He has clearly been openly and probably less openly on a larger scale financing and supporting terrorism among the Palestinians, and I suspect also aligning with those people—and this is important—who, one of the biggest obstacles to peace is not just the terrorism against Israelis, but the threats that arise against those Palestinians who want to make progress, so I think that is a help.

I think, as I said, the ability now of the moderate Arab countries to step up to the plate more easily is a help, but without any question, the commitment of the United States, the commitment of this President, the understanding that we have a major role to play, and I think that we have credibility in playing it that we did not have before.

The problem is incredibly difficult, let us not underestimate it, but I think the stakes are also huge. If two years from now, three years from now we could have the dual victories of a successful, prospering, free and democratic Iraq on the one hand, and a peace between Israelis and Palestinians on the other, those will be massive victories in the war against terrorism.

CHAFEE: Yes, I could not agree more, and seeing as how my light is still green, could you just reaffirm the President's commitment to the road map in these very, very difficult times as more than ever, with increased terrorist acts, the pressure to cease the settlements and to get the parties back talking about adhering to a road map?

WOLFOWITZ: Senator Chafee, you have heard him say it in public, I have heard him say it in private, and in circumstances where there was no need to reaffirm his commitment. He, I believe, *has understood from the beginning that it has got to be a major initiative coming off of a successful war in Iraq.*

CHAFEE: And my last question would be, there are those that question that commitment, and I suppose they want to see something accomplished on the settlement issue. What could you propose on that?

WOLFOWITZ: I think I will turn to my colleagues in the State Department. This is a very tough problem, but I heard Henry Kissinger put it in a way that I thought captured the issue rather well. *The Palestinians fear that Sharon is only prepared to grant them a shrunken kind of "Bantustan" sort of entity that would not be a state. The Israelis fear the Palestinians want a state only as a cease-fire and a stepping-stone to the destruction of Israel, and I think both sides need some reassurance.*

The Palestinians need some reassurance, which I think needs to come from us, that, in fact, the outcome is going to be a viable Palestinian state, and that obviously means the elimination of large areas of Israeli settlement activity, or at least a complete change in their status. At the same time, I think Israel needs the assurance that this really will be peace and not just a step on the way to something worse, and as I said, in this meeting with Europeans on the weekend, I think Europe needs to step up to the plate in terms of reassuring Israel. Both sides need reassurance, and outside parties I think have a big role to play now.

And finally, and I come back to my point about the Saudis, the Saudis in particular, but moderate Arab States in general, Egypt is important, could play a big role in part of that reassurance effort and also in, I think, encouraging the Palestinians to be reasonable on some of the more difficult issues.

It may be hard to appreciate today how refreshing this was in the spring of 2003. After all the prevarication in the run-up to the war, a high-ranking administration official was speaking candidly before a coequal branch of government.

The secretary told us that success in Iraq would help us strip Osama bin Laden of issues he was using against us. We had American troops stationed in Saudi Arabia to guard the Saudi monarchs against the threat of an invasion from the north ordered by Saddam. Osama bin Laden had used the presence of American troops near Mecca and Medina to great effect in inciting jihad against the West. President Bush had refused to address this troop presence as one of the motives behind bin Laden's campaign of terror. His administration and its surrogates in the media were quick to assail anyone who did. Mr. Wolfowitz understood the loaded cultural meaning of the word "crusade." He was the first to tell the Senate we could help defeat fanaticism by taking the "Crusaders in the Holy Land" issue away from Islamic radicals.

Naturally, we were all in favor of seeing democracy spread across the Arab world. Political oppression was a source of seething frustration there; if the cafes and markets were suddenly alive with free political discourse, it could only dampen the impulses that motivate extremism.

Finally, Mr. Wolfowitz underscored the critical connection between success in Iraq and success in building an Israeli-Palestinian peace—what he called "dual victories" in the war on terror. Still skeptical that the president was really committed to the establishment of a Palestinian state, I was encouraged by the correlation Mr. Wolfowitz had drawn. So far, all the president had done on the Israeli-Palestinian conflict was make a speech in the Rose Garden. Some of his predecessors in the White House had done serious work to bring Middle

Eastern leaders to the negotiating table—President Carter won the Nobel Peace Prize for his efforts, and President Clinton achieved a historic handshake between Prime Minister Yitzhak Rabin and Palestinian leader Yassir Arafat. Now, President Bush said he would chart a bold new direction in the peace process. Indeed his "road map" to a Palestinian state went far beyond any vision ever articulated by an American president.

I was a strong supporter of the land-for-peace principle, which amounts to Palestinians gaining a homeland in exchange for recognizing the legitimacy of the state of Israel and I was heartened by the Rose Garden speech. The president and I had battled over many issues but if he meant what he said about a Palestinian state, I would be one of his most vocal allies on the Senate Committee on Foreign Relations. I was in a key position now, as chairman of the subcommittee that has jurisdiction over our policy on the Israeli-Palestinian conflict. The preceding chairman, Republican senator Sam Brownback of Kansas, was irritated that under the Senate rules he had to give up the subcommittee chairmanship if he wanted to move up to the powerful Appropriations Committee. One day he asked me to let him have his cake and eat it, too. He asked me to step down voluntarily and allow him to continue running the subcommittee while still claiming the larger prize of Appropriations. Senator Brownback was agitated almost to the point of stamping his foot as he made his case. I refused to step down and urged him to abide by the Senate rules without complaint. I could not care less about the title; I was interested in results. I doubted that Senator Brownback would work as hard as I would on helping to establish a Palestinian state. Later that year, I would find out I was right.

Soon after we put the new committee assignments in place, Prime Minister Sharon said something curious in a January 27, 2003, interview with *Newsweek* magazine. President Bush had recently pledged that a quartet of world powers—the United States, the United Kingdom, Russia, and the United Nations—would keep his road map to peace on track. But in the *Newsweek* interview, here was Prime Minister Sharon inexplicably dismissing the importance of the quartet. "The quartet is nothing. Don't take it seriously," he said. "There is another plan that will work."

I was astonished. I am always ready to hear the facts as they are; I want honest talk, no matter how blunt. But when the Israeli prime minister brushed off the quartet, it was perplexing. Sharon had departed from the official script on how the president would make peace in the Middle East—the other half of the "dual" victory that Americans were dying for in Iraq.

The White House never challenged the Israeli leader's comments, and he never retracted them. They quickly faded from the news, but I was on my guard now. The president continued to make statements on the importance of his road map, as if Sharon had never publicly dismissed a key part of it.

A month later, on February 26, 2003, the president gave the road map the highest possible priority. He said when his impending war in Iraq was launched and won, peace between Israel and the Palestinians would have one less obstacle in its way. Months later, this speech, delivered before a friendly audience at the American Enterprise Institute, would assure me that Mr. Wolfowitz was not merely giving the Senate *his* opinion when he testified so expansively about the benefits expected to accrue from victory in Iraq.

In his speech at AEI, President Bush said, to applause, "Success in Iraq could also begin a new stage for Middle Eastern peace, and set in motion progress toward a truly democratic Palestinian state. For its part, the new government of Israel—as the terror threat is removed and security improves—will be expected to support the creation of a viable Palestinian state—and to work as quickly as possible toward a final status agreement. As progress is made toward peace, settlement activity in the occupied territories must end."

Then, in April, with the war under way, the State Department followed up on the president's two-state speech to AEI with a detailed, performance-based plan with concrete actions and a timeline. It was the first time his Rose Garden speech was codified and called "the road map." It set forth exactly what was required of Israel and the Palestinian Authority. The road map talked about "an independent, democratic and viable Palestinian state living side by side in peace and security with Israel." A final peace agreement would require Israel to withdraw from the West Bank and Gaza.

That same month, King Abdullah II of Jordan advised the White House to move quickly on the "dual-victories" strategy when Baghdad fell. In an interview on CNN, King Abdullah said, "People throughout the Middle East are very skeptical. The only way that you're going to make the right impression on the Arab street and throughout the region is to show there's going to be some transparency and solve the Israeli-Palestinian situation. If we don't move quickly, then everybody will say this [Iraq war] is just part of an agenda and there's a list of who's next." If the president was slow to act, he would lose all credibility as a broker of peace between Israel and the Palestinians.

And the president *did* appear to move quickly. On June 4, 2003, a week after Mr. Wolfowitz testified before the Committee on Foreign Relations, the president traveled to Aqaba, Jordan, to meet with King Abdullah, Ariel Sharon, and the Palestinian prime minister Mahmoud Abbas. The four world leaders stood shoulder to shoulder against the background of the sparkling Gulf of Aqaba, under swaying palms and an azure sky. When they spoke, each in turn seemed inspired by the beauty of the moment in that idyllic setting. It was a time of renewed hope.

The Israeli prime minister articulated his commitment to a Palestinian state in the West Bank. "It is in Israel's interest not to govern the Palestinians but for the Palestinians to govern themselves in their own state," Sharon said. "A democratic Palestinian state fully at peace with Israel will promote the long-term security and well-being of Israel as a Jewish state."

Abbas, speaking for the Palestinians, told Israel and the world, "Let me be very clear: There will be no military solution to this conflict, so we repeat our renunciation, a renunciation of terror against the Israelis wherever they might be."

Television images flashed around the world as the president declared that peace between Israel and the Palestinians was a top priority in the White House. He would send the respected ambassador John Wolf to Jerusalem as his special envoy, to work full time on achieving the terms of the road map.

"All here today now share a goal," the president said. "the Holy Land must be shared between the state of Palestine and the state of Israel, living at peace with each other and with every nation of the Middle East. All sides will benefit from this achievement and all sides have responsibilities to meet. As the road map accepted by the parties makes clear, both must make tangible immediate steps toward this two-state vision. . . .

"I've also asked Secretary of State Colin Powell, and National Security Adviser Condoleezza Rice, to make this cause a matter of the highest priority. Secretary Powell and Dr. Rice, as my personal representatives, will work closely with the parties, helping them move toward true peace as quickly as possible. The journey we're taking is difficult, but there is no other choice. No leader of conscience can accept more months and years of humiliation, killing and mourning. And these leaders of conscience have made their declarations today in the cause of peace."

As I watched the drama unfold and listened to these lofty words from my office in Washington, I thought, *This is a turning point. The president really is serious about a Palestinian state.*

After the Aqaba conference, Abbas called for Palestinian militants to observe a cease-fire, to adopt a *hudna,* a cooling-down period. We all hoped that if Abbas could show the Palestinians that a time of nonviolence would gain some measurable progress toward achieving their own state, the cease-fire might hold.

In the weeks to come, sadly, principal leaders responsible for progress on the road map ignored the issues that were most provocative to the Palestinians. Prime Minister Sharon was on record wholeheartedly endorsing a Palestinian state in the disputed territories, but Israel continued to build new settlements in the West Bank. It continued to erect a security wall that did not conform to the 1949 borders of the West Bank, the so-called Green Line. And it continued to hold Palestinian prisoners without charges.

Seven weeks after Aqaba, Israel was taking no discernable action to reward the nonviolence of the *hudna.* A desperate Mahmoud Abbas came to Washington to ask the president to get more involved in moving the peace process forward. He was not bringing the parties together in the ways that other presidents had, at Camp David, Wye River, Taba, and Sharm el-Sheikh.

Abbas met with the Senate Committee on Foreign Relations as well, pleading with us for help that would bolster his credibility. I heard the urgency in his voice: *If you intend to make peace and not just talk about it—strengthen me. Help me deliver for my people.*

After meeting with Abbas, President Bush made a statement at the White House, and, once again, said all the right things: "In our talks this morning, Prime Minister Abbas and I covered a range of issues. We discussed the impact on the Palestinian people of the limits on their freedom of movement and the need to reduce the network of checkpoints and barriers. Prime Minister Abbas shared his concerns about Israeli settlements, confiscation of land, and the building of a security fence. He also expressed his strong desire to see the release of many more Palestinian prisoners. We will continue to address these issues. We will address them carefully and seriously with Palestinian and Israeli officials. We will work to seek solutions."

Abbas went home with more promises, and the president

did nothing discernable to follow through. I was watching closely, and with growing frustration. Three weeks later, on August 19, a terrorist blew up a bus in Jerusalem, killing twenty innocent people. The attack marked the end of the *hudna,* and the end of Mahmoud Abbas as a credible alternative to Palestinian violence. Abbas resigned in despair on September 6. He told reporters that his "fundamental" reason for resigning was that Israel was unwilling to meet its commitments under the road map, and that the United States had failed to "exert sufficient influence" on Prime Minister Sharon.

I traveled to Israel shortly after the tragedy of the bombing. While there, I met with Ambassador Wolf, the special envoy the president had appointed with such fanfare at Aqaba. The ambassador and I spoke on the balcony of his suite at the King David Hotel in Jerusalem, overlooking the glorious Old City. I asked him to brief me on everything the Bush administration had done to strengthen Abbas and demonstrate that the Palestinians had much to gain by following him and everything to lose by murdering Israeli women and children.

Had the president acted on anything Abbas told him about the expanding settlements, the route of the security barrier, the thousands of prisoners jailed for years on end without charges?

Ambassador Wolf pursed his lips, shook his head, turned his palms up, and shrugged. I had my answer: We had done nothing. Later, the ambassador told reporters, "The administration failed to demand publicly that Israel and the Palestinians live up to their commitments as laid out in the plan known as the 'road map' to establish a Palestinian state."

What can explain the president's utter failure to even try to keep his promise on the road map? Why the inaction?

I found my answer in the West Bank, where Congressman Tom DeLay, Republican majority leader in the House, had once looked out and said, "I don't see occupied territory; I see Israel." I soon learned that Senator Sam Brownback, my predecessor as chairman of the subcommittee with oversight responsibility on Middle Eastern policy, was also in Jerusalem. We arranged to travel together for a day, sharing a security detail provided by the U.S. Embassy. On a memorable drive to Ramallah and back, we wound through the hilly West Bank, past roadblocks and scattered settlements. Senator Brownback railed against the scourge of Palestinian terrorism.

I said, "Sam, just theoretically, if the Palestinians were to cease all acts of violence for a year, or two years, or ten years, then could we talk about a Palestinian state in the West Bank and Gaza?"

My fellow politician did not waffle, wiggle, or duck, as so many do. He thought about my question, then turned to me with an honest and direct answer: "No."

That made me think about a rambling speech Senator James Inhofe of Oklahoma had given in the aftermath of September 11. He invoked his religious fervor when he proclaimed, of the war on terror, "Make no mistake about it, this war is first and foremost a spiritual war."

He went on to speak of the West Bank and Gaza, and insisted that Israel must never yield this "promised land" to Palestinians. Why?

"Because God said so," Senator Inhofe declared. "In Genesis, the Bible says: 'The Lord said to Abram, "Lift up now your eyes, and look from the place where you are northward, and southward, and eastward and westward; for all the land which you see, to you will I give it, and to your seed forever . . ." ' This is God talking," the senator said. "This is not a political battle at all. It is a contest over whether or not the Word of God is true."

Like Senator Brownback—and perhaps even President Bush—Senator Inhofe believes the Palestinians have no claim to the West Bank and Gaza.

I respect deeply held beliefs, but government leaders must never allow their religious beliefs to interfere with American diplomacy. I would think this question was behind us. Senator John F. Kennedy addressed it in 1960 when he declared that the pope would not influence American foreign policy if the voters put a Catholic in the White House.

Certainly, no religious group in America speaks in a monolithic voice. Some Christians who read the Bible as literally as Sam Brownback and Jim Inhofe believe God would be pleased to see Israel negotiate with its Palestinian brothers and sisters and share the Promised Land.

As a political stance, the concept of no-land-for-peace can only point the way to more bloodshed. Without a Palestinian homeland, the future is one of endless occupation and intifada, a struggle that both the Israelis and the Palestinians seem destined to lose.

I was by no means alone in this thinking. By the fall of 2003, the many Israelis and Palestinians who wanted to live together in peace had grown frustrated and disillusioned with President Bush's hollow words on the road map. They took matters into their own hands.

Israelis and Palestinians met informally in Geneva, Switzerland, outside the channels of government, to push for some urgency in the search for peace. On October 12, 2003, they produced a "draft framework" on how officials might be able to implement the two-state solution. They meant to put the spotlight back on the road map as a policy that might yet be salvaged. The letter transmitting what came to be known as the Geneva Accords said:

"At this point in time, after the Palestinian government and the Israeli government have accepted the Road Map, which includes reaching a final-status settlement by 2005, based on a two-state solution, we consider it to be of the utmost importance to present to the two peoples and the entire world an example of what such a final status agreement could include. This is proof that despite all the pain entailed in concessions, it is possible to reach a historical compromise which meets the vital national interests of each side."

The Geneva Accords spelled out how Israelis and Palestinians might achieve reconciliation on the most difficult core issues: the borders of the West Bank and the right of Palestinians to return to their ancestral properties.

The Geneva framework was imperfect, but, without question, it had advanced the cause of peace. It was an extraordinary turn of events: Ordinary citizens had seized the initiative that their governments had lost—or perhaps never intended to pursue. I admired these efforts and thought they represented the kind of free and open democratic process we were ostensibly trying to sell to the Arab world when we invaded Iraq.

When the Geneva signatories came to Washington to promote their fifty-page framework for peace, Secretary of State

Colin Powell and Deputy Secretary Paul Wolfowitz agreed to meet with them. Prime Minister Sharon's deputy, Ehud Olmert, who would later succeed him, did much to prevent those meetings when he denounced them as "a mistake."

Olmert told reporters that Powell would undermine the road map if he met with Israeli and Palestinian peace activists. A call went to the White House, no doubt, and soon Powell was saying he was unavailable to meet. The authors of the Geneva Accords had offered up a potential peace deal from the grass roots, the source of all power in any democratic system; they were met with criticism, and even scorn. Without explanation, Mr. Wolfowitz also canceled his meeting with the Geneva signatories. It was understood in Washington that pressure had come from the White House. I took it as one more sign that in the Bush-Cheney era, the eagle on our national seal had both talons chockful of arrows; there was no power to be had in wielding an olive branch.

It was clear to me that Secretary Wolfowitz had wanted to meet with the framers of the Geneva Accord. He had talked about peace when I asked him about the ripples emanating from the rock we had thrown into the pool by invading Iraq. He was glad to define "victory" as winning the peace without firing a shot. We needed to get "dual victories" out of the war in Iraq if we were serious about combating terrorism, he said. I was encouraged, then, that at least someone high up in the administration thought the peace process was important.

The effort in Geneva was not the only grassroots movement aimed at pushing the American and Israeli governments beyond words and toward action. "The People's Voice," a petition drive headed by Palestinian scholar Sari Nusseibeh and

Israeli war hero Ami Ayalon, collected 100,000 Israeli signatures and 60,000 Palestinian signatures in support of the languishing road map.

In a speech at Georgetown University on October 30, 2003, Mr. Wolfowitz said the petition drive was a positive development. "One of the keys to achieving peace is to somehow mobilize majorities on both sides so the extremists who oppose it can be isolated," he said. He was talking sense, but the clashists who ran the administration went to work criticizing him.

There were other Americans demanding a more determined effort. Prominent evangelical leaders started to take President Bush to task for his false promises on peace. Like Mr. Wolfowitz, they understood the vital connection between peace in the holy land and the war in Iraq—a war that was starting to look more like a colossal failure by the day.

On December 2, 2003, a day after the Geneva Accords were signed, I attended a remarkable meeting at the National Press Club in Washington. Jewish, Christian, and Muslim leaders were there to launch what they called a National Interreligious Leadership Initiative. Reverend Mark S. Hanson, presiding bishop of the Evangelical Lutheran Church in America, said, "The perilous lack of progress on the Road Map leaves us rightfully impatient. Doubts about the seriousness of the United States' commitment to the Road Map must be replaced by the evidence of the strong leadership we witnessed from President Bush and his administration last spring." I assumed he was referring to the conference in Aqaba, Jordan, in June 2003.

All of us present shared Mr. Hanson's doubts about whether the White House was serious about the road map.

There was no evidence whatsoever that might suggest a good-faith effort aimed at building the peace. The road map expressly barred either side from taking any unilateral action, on any issue. In Aqaba, President Bush reinforced that principle. He declared that "no unilateral actions by either side can or should prejudge the outcome of future negotiations." When the Geneva Accords and the People's Voice started to gain attention, Deputy Prime Minister Olmert announced that Israel would unilaterally withdraw from the occupied Gaza Strip. He declared that since there was no negotiated agreement in place at that time, "we need to implement a unilateral alternative." This unilateral dismantling of settlements in Gaza was a brazen flouting of the road map. Where was President Bush?

At Aqaba, he had declared that the quartet of world powers, the United States, the United Kingdom, Russia, and the United Nations, would use all their power to keep Israel and the Palestinians on the road map to a Palestinian state living side-by-side in peace with Israel. I doubted that the United Kingdom, Russia, or the United Nations had been consulted before Ohmert announced the plan to disengage from Gaza. Prime Minister Sharon was right earlier that year when he told *Newsweek,* "The quartet is nothing, don't take it seriously. There is another plan that will work."

Without a hint of criticism from the White House, the Sharon government was shredding the road map before our eyes. Meanwhile calls from the Arab world for U.S. leadership on the road map became more and more urgent in the ensuing months.

Syrian president Hafez Assad said, "We in Syria believe that if the United States doesn't have the vision and the will to make peace in the Middle East, everything else will lose its value and there is going to be no peace.

"We see that the only solution is for Israel to withdraw from Arab-occupied territories and to dismantle the settlements. And this is consistent with what you have said about the vision of President Bush to have a two-state solution and to have peace in the region."

Again, King Abdullah of Jordan came to Washington to meet with President Bush and urge him to do something—anything—to show progress on the road map. In a speech on April 4, 2004, Abdullah said, "I can't impress it enough on this audience that the core instability of the Middle East, the core problem in everybody's hearts, is the Israeli-Palestinian problem. That is the recruiting ground for extremism and terrorism that we see in the Middle East."

A week later, Egyptian president Hosni Mubarak went to Crawford, Texas, to meet with the president and urge him to act. That would be the only way to restore confidence in the process. "The United States has always assumed a leading role in the search for peace in our region. I expressed my strong desire to see that this leading role continue, with ever greater vigor and determination to realize our vision of a two-state solution," President Mubarak said.

"I expressed to the president the centrality of the conflict to the people of the region," he said.

Three regional leaders, friend and foe alike, had told our president that solving the Israeli-Palestinian conflict was important to achieving stability in a region where Americans were increasingly perceived as occupiers and crusaders.

Two days later, in what I considered a sharp rebuke to

these entreaties, President Bush wrote a letter to Prime Minister Sharon effectively abandoning the peace process.

"In light of new realities on the ground," he wrote, "including already existing major Israeli population centers, it is unrealistic to expect that the outcome of final status negotiations will be a full and complete return to the armistice lines of 1949, and all previous efforts to negotiate a two-state solution have reached the same conclusion." The president declared that the Green Line of 1949 was no longer on the table for Israelis and Palestinians to negotiate.

In that April 14, 2004, letter, the president undercut everything he had said with such fanfare in the Rose Garden. He brazenly kept up the rhetoric, but made it clear that on his watch, there would be no "viable and contiguous" Palestinian state. The peace that Anwar Sadat, Yitzhak Rabin, and so many others had died for would remain a distant dream.

In my mind, the new reality on the ground was that President Bush was finally finished with another charade. He had never intended to preside over the founding of a Palestinian homeland in the West Bank. He was now, on the record, turning his back on that pledge.

Where was Congress all this time?

In 1999, on one of my first days in the Senate chamber, Republican senator Slade Gorton motioned to me during a lull in the day's business. *I want to talk to you.* I had no idea whether it was about Senate business or the political campaign I faced, or if he just wanted to welcome me to Washington. I stood, buttoned my suit jacket, and walked over. I recognized him because when he was campaigning for the Senate in 1980 I was shoeing horses on the harness-racing circuit in Alberta,

Canada. Cable television in Calgary carried channels out of Spokane, Washington, and I had watched a lot of Slade Gorton for Senate ads.

That day in the Senate chamber, he said, *Linc, I want to give you some advice. Your father didn't always support the AIPAC agenda. I don't think you want to follow on that same path.*

He waited for my reaction.

I thought, *These are the first words of advice from a colleague in the United States Senate?*

I knew the organization he was talking about, the American-Israeli Public Affairs Committee, one of the most powerful and successful lobbying organizations in America. We share an ardent support for the bond between the United States and Israel. I, too, believe the security of the State of Israel is not negotiable, and I would attend innumerable AIPAC meetings in my Senate tenure. The group was always welcome in my office, as was the Israel Policy Forum or Brit Tzedek v'Shalom or Peace Now or any other advocacy group.

I resented Senator Gorton's advice. No United States senator should be a marionette. As I would do many times over the next seven years in Washington, I checked my temper, held my tongue, nodded appreciatively, and thanked the distinguished gentleman, as they say.

On June 23 and 24, 2004, the Senate debated a resolution endorsing the president's April 14 letter, the one that had cited "new realitics on the ground" in the West Bank. It was troubling to me how quiet Congress had been on the subject of the road map for the past two years, but now senators stood ready to support a complete departure from it. There were certainly new realities on the ground in Iraq that no one wanted to recognize—a growing insurgency, the outbreak of sectarian civil war—but the attention of the Congress was focused on telling the Palestinians that if they ever achieved a homeland it would indeed be the patchwork Bantustan they had feared.

With the Senate poised to vote on the New Realities letter, I pondered the wisdom of opposing the resolution before us. Would it be understood that I believed the letter meant the end of the road map or anything like it, and thus was not in Israel's best interest?

With so few voices in Congress willing to debate this emotional issue, I concluded that voting against the resolution would be misinterpreted. I did not want to create yet another side controversy that would distract us from the real task at hand—to make progress on peace. I decided to vote yea, but I made a statement for the *Congressional Record* expressing my concern about this diversion. Over time I had come to understand Senator Gorton's warning and cast a vote I regret.

In the fall of 2004, as I brooded over the tragic disconnect between the Bush-Cheney administration's high-sounding rhetoric and its failure to act, I read a disturbing interview with Dov Weisglass, chief of staff to Sharon. Weisglass was the Israeli prime minister's closest adviser and had been at his side for decades. He was astonishingly blunt in his conversation with the Israeli news organization *Haaretz*. His comments, so strongly worded and full of conviction, were impossible to dismiss.

Weisglass told the world that the road map had been a ruse from the start. Sharon himself had said as much in *Newsweek* nineteen months earlier, when he divulged, "There is another plan that will work."

Asked why Israel had violated the road map by unilaterally disengaging from Gaza, Weisglass said, "The significance of the disengagement plan is the freezing of the peace process. . . . And when you freeze that process, you prevent the establishment of a Palestinian state, and you prevent a discussion on the refugees, the borders and Jerusalem. Effectively, this whole package called the Palestinian state, with all that it entails, has been removed indefinitely from our agenda."

"The disengagement is actually formaldehyde," he said. "It supplies the amount of formaldehyde that is necessary so there will not be a political process with the Palestinians."

In the fall of 2003, Weisglass said, top officials in both governments knew there would be no Palestinian state.

"We understood that everything is stuck," he said. "And even though according to the Americans' reading of the situation, the blame fell on the Palestinians and not on us, Arik [Prime Minister Sharon] grasped that this state of affairs would not last. That they wouldn't leave us alone, wouldn't get off our case. Time was not on our side. There was international erosion, internal erosion. Domestically, in the meantime, everything was collapsing. The economy was stagnant, and the Geneva Initiative garnered broad support. And then we were hit with letters of officers and letters of pilots and letters of commandos [letters of refusal to serve in the territories]. These were not weird kids with green ponytails and a ring in their nose who give off a strong odor of grass. These were people like Spector's group [Yiftah Spector, a renowned air force pilot who signed the pilot's letter]. Really our finest young people."

Chillingly, Weisglass cited the vote we had in Congress in June, on endorsing the president's "new realities on the ground" letter. He said the resolution proved that the United States was openly supporting Israel in preventing the establishment of a Palestinian state in the West Bank. "Today that same approach guides the president of the United States," Weisglass said. And he had the numbers at his fingertips. "It was passed in the House of Representatives by a vote of 405–7, and in the Senate by 95–5."

The vote in the Senate had been 95–3, with two absent. I thought it was telling that Weisglass had counted the two absent senators as voting with the opposition.

Weisglass said out loud what I and other skeptics had deduced from the evidence: There was no commitment to the road map. I thought, here is a man as honest as Senator Sam Brownback and Senator Jim Inhofe. Finally, some truth! Weisglass was so stark in contradicting the official line on the road map that I immediately called Secretary Wolfowitz to ask whether he still thought peace between Israel and the Palestinians was one of the "dual victories" we were fighting for in the president's war on terror. I reached Paul while he was thirty-five thousand feet over the Atlantic, returning to Washington after a trip to Europe. He said he was unaware of the Weisglass interview, and then quickly went on to discount it. The comments must have been intended for a domestic audience in Israel, to placate a faction in the government, he said. I doubted that. The statement was far too detailed, even shocking. I went by the text in front of me and concluded that Dov Weisglass had wandered off the duplicitous script that other officials involved in the road map were following. People who enjoy manipulating world events also seem to enjoy bragging about the power they wield behind the scenes. I was grateful to Weisglass for his candor. His comments reinforced the conclusions I had drawn from all available evidence, the same conclusions reached by the authors of the Geneva Accords, the People's Voice, the Reverend Mark Hanson, and others.

Weisglass had all but crowed that the road map was a deliberate deception. His disclosures had cemented my cynicism about the Bush-Cheney policy in the Middle East.

In October 2003 I crossed the West Bank into Jordan with Republican senators Mitch McConnell, Conrad Burns, Craig Thomas, and Larry Craig. As we bounced along in a van through that hardscrabble territory, two lines from "Peace in the Valley" rolled through my head:

> *"There will be peace in the valley for me, some day*
> *There will be peace in the valley for me, oh Lord I pray."*

I knew Johnny Cash's version of the old spiritual, a song with roots in the Book of Isaiah. I mentioned it to my colleagues, just to see them roll their eyes. We were among Republicans, as in the caucus, where senators were used to me speaking up and coming at an issue from a different angle. When I mentioned "Peace in the Valley," Conrad burst into song.

> *"Well the bear will be gentle*
> *And the wolves will be tame*
> *And the lion shall lay down by the lamb, oh yes*

And the beasts of the wild
Shall be lit by a child
And I'll be changed, changed from this creature that I am,
   oh yes."

He knew every word. It made for a lighthearted moment in an otherwise grim trip across terrain that has seen centuries of strife. Conrad continued to sing as we rumbled along, and I wondered if the world leaders talking about peace in *this* valley really meant to bring it about.

Despite the discouraging events of 2003 and 2004—the continuing pattern of Palestinian violence, Israeli intransigence, and White House inaction—the spring of 2005 brought yet another opportunity to heal old wounds.

With the death of Yassir Arafat on November 11, 2004, the Palestinians held new elections to choose a successor. The elections were free and fair and included even the most radical parties. In the end, a hopeful Palestinian people chose Mahmoud Abbas, the moderate who had pleaded with Washington in 2003, that summer of "Mission Accomplished," to strengthen his hand. Turnout was high, and that gave Abbas a strong mandate as president of the Palestinian Authority. I was astonished that the Palestinians were willing, once again, to trust the White House. They still believed that President Bush meant to follow through; that his Rose Garden speech on a Palestinian state living side by side with Israel in peace and security, was more than just words. I wished I could believe along with them, but I feared the president would again shatter the trust of Israelis and Palestinians who were sincerely working for peace. As an American, it broke my heart to know we were probably going to fail these people.

I no longer believed the president when he said, on February 22, 2005, not long after Abbas was elected, "Israel must freeze settlement activity, help Palestinians build a thriving economy, and ensure that a new Palestinian state is truly viable, with contiguous territory on the West Bank. A state of scattered territories will not work."

It was a plan he would do nothing to implement or promote. The only difference was that this time no special presidential envoy would be sent to Jerusalem to turn his palms up and shrug in despair when nothing happened.

Predictably, within five months, President Abbas was back at the White House to beseech President Bush for help in quelling the unrest in the disputed territories. Abbas was desperate to shore up the moderate political support so recently expressed in the Palestinian elections.

On June 1, 2005, a week after his meeting with President Bush, *The Wall Street Journal* published a column written by Abbas. His sense of urgency and even anger were evident. "Every day, Israel is undertaking steps that undermine President Bush's vision and effectively preclude a two-state solution to the Israeli-Palestinian conflict," Abbas wrote.

> Israel's ongoing settlement construction in the West Bank, its insidious Wall which, since not built on the 1967 border, is suffocating Palestinian cities and towns, and its illegal attempts to cut off East Jerusalem from the rest of the West Bank will, if allowed to continue, render a two-state solution to our conflict an impossibility. If the two-state solution dies, our democracy cannot be far behind, for

democracy and freedom are intertwined: It is impossible to have one without the other.

Time is the greatest enemy of peace in the Middle East. And the time for interim agreements and partial accords is over. It is no longer enough to simply manage the conflict while Israel unilaterally acts. For the sake of peace and democracy, it is time to end the conflict. Israelis and Palestinians now have an opportunity to do just that—to bring a permanent end to our tragic conflict. I am ready immediately to sit down with Ariel Sharon and start permanent peace negotiations. When I meet with President Bush today, I will ask him to fulfill his vision of two sovereign, viable, democratic states, living side-by-side in peace and security. If he is still convinced and committed to his original vision, as I hope he will be, and if Prime Minister Sharon is pressed to abandon a unilateral solution, we can together make 2005 the year of peace in the Middle East.

The United States should have done everything possible to bolster this strong voice for peace. After meeting with Abbas, President Bush once again made a forceful statement calling for an end to the expansion of Israeli settlements in the West Bank. And that was *all* he did. There was no intensive diplomatic effort to back up the statement.

We would soon reap what we had sown in the Middle East. When the Palestinian people held parliamentary elections in January 2006, they were tired of following this deceptive road map. They elected candidates backed by Hamas—a violent organization with a genocidal charter—to a majority in the 132-seat Palestinian Legislative Council.

When Paul Wolfowitz outlined what was at stake, how the war on terror hinged on "dual victories," it was no passing fancy; it was a solid analysis that held true as the years passed. In 2006, the bipartisan Iraq Study Group made the exact same connection between the war in Iraq and peace between Israel and the Palestinians. It was a very different environment then, of course. The conduct of the war was recognized around the world as a fiasco. With the president focused on *Stay the course,* Congress created the Iraq Study Group to assess the dire situation in Iraq and recommend the changes we needed to adopt in order to succeed. James Baker and Lee Hamilton led a panel that included some of the most sober-minded and thoughtful figures in American public life. They had earned the confidence of six presidents, four of them Republican. When I saw this distinguished bipartisan roster and its deep experience in war and peace, I thought, *These are people we can trust.* Lawrence Eagleburger worked in the Nixon administration and became secretary of state under President George H. W. Bush; Edwin Meese was chief of staff to Governor Ronald Reagan, then attorney general to President Ronald Reagan; William Perry was secretary of defense to President Clinton. These were people not likely to cut and run.

The White House may have been mired in denial but the Iraq Study Group confronted the war head-on and grappled with it. Its report was unflinching from the very first sentence: "The situation in Iraq is grave and deteriorating."

The group stressed that the United States "will not be able to achieve its goals in the Middle East unless the United States deals directly with the Arab-Israeli conflict."

"There must be a renewed and sustained commitment by the United States to a comprehensive Arab-Israeli peace on all fronts," they reported. "The United States does its ally Israel no favors in avoiding direct involvement to solve the Arab-Israeli conflict."

The report urged the president to start talking to the Iranians and Syrians. "Given the ability of Iran and Syria to influence events within Iraq and their interest in avoiding chaos in Iraq, the United States should try to engage them constructively."

Some Republicans, driven by both politics and conscience, started to rebel. Senator Gordon Smith of Oregon withdrew his support for President Bush's Iraq war.

On the Senate floor, he said, "I, for one, am at the end of my rope when it comes to supporting a policy that has our soldiers patrolling the same streets in the same way, being blown up by the same bombs, day after day. That is absurd. It may *even be criminal.*"

But the defections were too few. Lawmakers continued to "support the troops" by writing the president a blank check; they allowed him to feed more human beings into the meat grinder while Congress worked the political calculations, making sure that failure in Iraq, when it finally came, would belong to President Bush alone. This Congress deserves the infamy that history will surely assign it.

When the Bush-Cheney administration had no further use for Paul Wolfowitz, he was moved to the World Bank. He had gone off script one time too often. In May 2003, shortly before he answered my rock-in-the-pool question with his "dual victories" formula, he suggested to *Vanity Fair* that the administration had many unstated reasons for invading Iraq but got the public on board by talking almost exclusively about weapons of mass destruction.

"The truth is that for reasons that have a lot to do with the U.S. government bureaucracy, we settled on the one issue that everyone could agree on, which was weapons of mass destruction as the core reason," he said.

Mr. Wolfowitz summed up the Bush-Cheney policy in the region thus: "I think the two most important things next are the two most obvious. One is getting post-Saddam Iraq right. Getting it right may take years, but setting the conditions for getting it right in the next six months . . . The next six months are going to be very important. The other thing is trying to get some progress on the Israeli-Palestinian issue."

When I read that, I thought back to how EPA administrator Christie Todd Whitman had made the mistake of taking President Bush at his word. In her public appearances, she often repeated his campaign pledge on regulating greenhouse gases. I think she believed him. But remember that just weeks into the new administration, Vice President Cheney delighted the Republican caucus by announcing that the president had no intention of honoring that pledge. A senator shouted, "Somebody better tell Christie!" as the caucus erupted with cheers.

On the president's road map to peace, I was left thinking, *Somebody better tell Wolfowitz.*

19

THE FUTURE

As the Bush administration grinds to a welcome constitutional end, the Republican and Democratic parties remain entrenched at the political extremes. Republicans have led poorly and Democrats have shown themselves unable to lead at all. Neither party inspires confidence in its ability to unite America and repair what has been damaged at home and abroad.

If one or both parties do not start heeding the center, the voters will make a tectonic shift in politics on their own. They will leave their most partisan fellow citizens behind, in ever-shrinking tents of red and blue.

I believe this is the way forward in American politics: centrist Americans, disenchanted with Republicans and Democrats alike, coalescing around third-party candidates who are focused on the future; on solving, not exploiting, the problems we face, whether those problems were thrust upon us by others, or we foolishly brought them on ourselves.

A centrist movement was under construction in the late 1990s in reaction to the incessant feuding between House Republicans and the Democratic president. The rancor shut down the government for a time and mired us in the impeachment of President Clinton over prevarications that now seem trivial, given the monumental ones we hear from his successor.

In January 2001, when Republican senators met in a biennial retreat at the Library of Congress, pollster John Zogby told us that after decades of tracking voter trends, he was certain of one unavoidable fact: The only Americans who delight in partisan bickering are the partisans at the extremes; most Americans live in "the vital center" and want their politicians to start listening to reason.

"There is a burgeoning centrist third party waiting to be formed," Zogby told us. "If either party moves too much toward its core base on the right or the left, it can open the center up to exploitation by the other party. Or, if neither party reads the tea leaves wisely, the center can open up to this new party."

This was seven years ago, when America still believed that President-elect George W. Bush would unite us at the center, as he had promised when asking for our votes. Since then, America has endured his destabilization of the Middle East; suspension of the writ of habeas corpus; retreat from the Geneva conventions' ban on torture; repudiation of the Fourth Amendment guarantee against warrantless searches; and relentless demagoguery on the flag, abortion, and gays. The president leaves the country exponentially more divided than he found it. The opportunity for the emergence of a third party is greater than ever.

Major political parties may seem like permanent fixtures in the civic landscape; but, like all things, they rise and fall and pass into history. I believe the rise of a credible third party, when it happens, will hurt Democrats more than Republicans. The Republican base is strong and rallying behind its ramparts. It is kicking out moderates and vowing never to change. It will crawl over broken glass to support an extreme Republican agenda.

On the other hand, the Democratic base is demoralized by its failed presidential campaigns of 2000 and 2004 and by the congressional Democratic leadership's complicity in the Iraq War debacle. I would not be surprised to see mass defections of Democratic voters when a legitimate third party begins to gain attention.

The next mass movement of American voters may come out of an existing party apparatus, such as the Greens or the Libertarians; but it seems more likely to gather around a personality first, then a platform. That was how enthusiasm started to build around independent presidential candidates John Anderson in 1980 and H. Ross Perot in 1992.

When a third way mounts a serious challenge to the Republican and Democratic parties, I suspect it will come out of nowhere and gather strength with surprising speed. The Republican Party had existed for only two years when it ran a credible race for president in 1856. It won eleven states that year, drawing on mass defections from the disintegrating Whig Party. The fledgling Republicans won the White House just four years later, in 1860. There were four candidates in the race that year, and all were strong enough to win states. Nonetheless, Abraham Lincoln won the presidency by capturing 180 votes in the Electoral College. That was a comfortable twenty-eight-vote margin of victory at the time. Interestingly, the nation's first Republican president won without a single electoral vote from the South, now the stronghold of the Republican Party. The future Great Emancipator was not even on the ballot in most southern states.

Was this kind of dramatic upheaval in presidential politics more possible in Lincoln's day than our own? To be sure, campaigns were not saturated with money and mass-media advertising in 1860. Then again, there was no Internet. Today's technology may be leveling the field in ways we cannot fully grasp yet.

If the next Lincoln fails to win the 270 Electoral College votes needed to attain the presidency, and, at the same time, denies victory to the Republican or the Democrat, the House of Representatives will step in and elect a president. The process is governed by the Twelfth Amendment to the Constitution, ratified in 1804, and the Twentieth Amendment, ratified in 1933.

In 1825, the House elected John Quincy Adams to the presidency after the election failed to award the requisite number of Electoral College votes to one of the four candidates on the ballot. Andrew Jackson had won the popular vote and more Electoral College votes than any other candidate. Jackson's supporters accused insiders in the House of stealing the election.

A similar crisis loomed 143 years later, in 1968, when George Wallace, the segregationist governor of Alabama, almost caused a "contingent election" in the House. His third-party campaign for president, in a time torn by race and an unpopular foreign war, carried five Southern states with forty-six electoral votes. If Wallace had taken just thirty-two additional Electoral College votes from Richard Nixon, the House would have elected a president that year.

Times of political renewal are uncertain ones. If no party is strong enough to win in the Electoral College, the Constitution gives each state's House delegation a single vote to cast for president. Under that one-state one-vote system, the lone House member from Alaska has the same voice as all fifty-three members representing California. There are seven states—Alaska, Delaware, Montana, North Dakota, South Dakota, Vermont, and Wyoming—that have only one representative in the House. That puts a mere seven lawmakers out of 435 in control of 14 percent of the vote; these lone delegates for their respective states wield enormous power in a nation that often elects a president by a razor-thin margin. At the same time, they may safeguard against the House electing a president who has strong support in only a handful of states.

Other aspects of the two Constitutional amendments seem to embrace uncertainty. Every House member would be a free agent in arguing how his or her delegation should cast its single vote. Every delegation would collectively be free to decide whether to acknowledge the popular vote or to frustrate it. Even in a state where citizens voted overwhelmingly for the third-party challenger, the House delegation could cast its vote for the spurned Republican or Democrat instead. Politically, House members would be under extraordinary pressure to do just that—to give power to one of their own.

Any enthusiasm that Americans have for organizing a major third party must be tempered by this cold reality: Its birth pangs may bring about a constitutional crisis in which no one can foresee the outcome.

The contingency election of 1825 played out in the political arena, but given our more litigious nature in the modern era, we could count on legions of partisan lawyers swarming into Washington. They would battle over every shade of meaning in the text of the Twelfth and Twentieth amendments. A potential for stalemate exists. In 1825, after days of debate, the House wrote "rules of procedure" to govern its election of the sixth president of the United States. A modern House might look to those rules as a guide, but would not be bound by them. It is entirely possible the crisis would be resolved in the United States Supreme Court instead of the House, and that, ominously, is where the past becomes prologue.

In 2001, in the Library of Congress, Mr. Zogby told our Republican Senate caucus that voters wanted a return to the center. "This is one of those times that call for giants who can read the national mood," he said. Seven years later, we know that the forty-third president of the United States was not that giant. On his watch, American voters succumbed to the politics of fear in 2002, and again in 2004; but they never lost their instinct for the unifying center. In 2006 they showed that America can regain its footing quickly, even after the shock of an event as unprecedented and world changing as September 11.

When a credible third party gathers strength, we should make it a part of our political culture to ask House candidates whether they would respect the will of the people or whether they would go their own way if called upon to elect a president.

They would be free to break their pledges, obviously. But some will honor their pledges, too. It is worth getting them on the record, if only to give them the cover they need to resist Republican and Democratic demands for a partisan vote.

There is great political danger in allowing the House to frustrate the will of the voters. The system works best when power remains in the hands of the voters. I was a casualty of the system working in 2006, and while defeat is never easy, I give the voters credit: They made the connection between re-electing even popular Republicans at the cost of leaving the Senate in the hands of a leadership they had learned to mistrust. In Rhode Island, Montana, Virginia, Missouri, Pennsylvania, and Ohio, the voters did what they had to do to check the Bush-Cheney agenda. But that does not mean they will continue to tolerate the abysmal leadership of the new Democratic majority in the House and Senate.

Ultimately, we can have complete faith in the American voters; they have proven themselves time and time again. When history demands it, I believe they will make the leap to a new political order—without a vote in the House if they can, with a vote if they must. In the 1968 race for president, an insurgent candidate who pandered to fear and racism put a scare into the major parties when he carried five states with forty-six electoral votes. I believe that a centrist movement appealing to the best in America, not the worst, will be all the stronger for it. The political center, when it arises, will lead the way to a truly great American era.

Index